55 Teaching Dilemmas

Ten powerful solutions to almost any classroom challenge

Kathy Paterson

Pembroke Publishers Limited

© **2005** Pembroke Publishers
538 Hood Road
Markham, Ontario, Canada L3R 3K9
www.pembrokepublishers.com

Distributed in the U.S. by Stenhouse Publishers
480 Congress Street
Portland, ME 04101-3400
www.stenhouse.com

We acknowledge the financial support of the Government of Canada through the Book
Publishing Industry Development Program (BPIDP) for our publishing activities.

We acknowledge the Government of Ontario through the Ontario Media Development
Corporation.

Library and Archives Canada Cataloguing in Publication

Paterson, Kathy
    55 teaching dilemmas : ten powerful solutions to almost any classroom
challenge / Kathy Paterson.

Includes index.
ISBN 1-55138-191-5

    1. Elementary school teaching. I. Title. II. Title: Fifty-five teaching dilemmas.

LB1025.3.P378 2005   372.1102   C2005-903312-6

Printed and bound in Canada
9 8 7 6 5 4 3 2 1

Contents

Introduction
The Power We Have as Teachers

Teachers aspire to teach well, but reaching this commendable goal is not always easy. Striving for it requires strength, energy, and might, as well as the vital ability to influence others, especially the students. First-rate teachers have the inner traits and influential abilities needed and use them together with well-thought-through teaching strategies. They dare to be powerful in their pursuit of excellence, and to use their strengths to benefit their students.

I will never forget one professor's demonstration of teacher power. The professor calmly faced his large class of education students and said solemnly, "Please follow my directions exactly." The class listened attentively. "Put your finger on your nose," he said. When all the students immediately complied—he *was* their instructor, after all—he continued. "Put your other hand on your head and stick out your tongue." He paused, smiled slightly, and said: "How silly you all look! See how much power a teacher has. You all blindly followed where I led. Remember that when you are teaching young minds much less sophisticated than yours."

Yes, as teachers, we have the power that comes from our position, but also the potential, maybe the ability, to teach dynamically, passionately, and well, and by so doing influence our students, the shapers of the future. Surely, nothing can be more important than that!

A Daunting Responsibility

With such tremendous influence, though, comes much responsibility. What if we teach a concept incorrectly? What if we inadvertently "turn a student off"? What if we say something that a child misconstrues and takes as an insult or personal attack? How can we possibly say the right things and act in the right ways all the time? We may find the responsibility we face truly daunting.

It is not uncommon for even the best of educators to second-guess their abilities, cross-examine their weaknesses, and critically judge their capabilities as teachers. They wonder whether they have the traits, skills, and strategies to teach in our fast-paced, technological world. Maybe you have similar doubts.

Let me assure you that, with a little polishing, you already have what it takes to teach with excellence. You already have the basic skills and personality; otherwise, you wouldn't be reading this book. Perhaps what you need is to hone your personal traits and professional strategies. You will then be better able to help your students flower as individuals and as learners. You will be more confident in your overall abilities and less upset by unavoidable human errors. You will be a more powerful teacher with power over yourself and over your teaching abilities positively reflected in your students.

Every day, teachers exhibit personal strengths and practise good teaching strategies in the classroom. We reach children by instructing, modelling, and leading from our hearts and souls, using every tool, resource, and personal skill available to us. At our best, we are successful communicators, influential role models, first-rate educators who teach with power and excellence.

Interwoven Strengths

Although the concept of teaching excellence is simple—effective, time-efficient, child-centred teaching—the elements that contribute to it are vast and multifaceted. For the purpose of this book, these fundamentals could be contained in two major areas: personal power and professional power. Even within these broad categories that encompass many kinds of strength, the traits and strategies overlap. That is because excellent teaching is a tightly woven union of personal characteristics and instructional style, resulting in great academic success and personal growth for both students and teachers. Students will be happy, confident, able to handle curriculum well, and eager to learn; teachers will be pleased with the work of their charges and confident in their own strengths and teaching abilities.

The ability to teach well and influence others comes from within. It is more than an exercise of techniques taught in teacher education classes. It is more than efficient time management within a crowded curriculum. And it is reflected in more than a well-behaved, disciplined class. Teaching well is like kindling a flame and watching it blossom, creating learners who are so excited about learning that they seem to grow right before the teacher's eyes. These fortunate students can hardly wait for the school day to begin and never want class to end. These are students whose teachers exhibit both personal and professional power.

I do not think that teachers can show professional power without first having personal power. *Personal power* might be defined as control over who they are, how they interact with others, what personae they present to the students, and what their philosophy of education is. *Professional power* refers to excellence in instructing, leading, and influencing. It might be seen as power over teaching abilities, the effective use of strategies that encourage and support learning.

I believe that teachers who have personal power present personalities that are both positive and supportive and will see this reflected in the behavior of their students. Similarly, teachers with professional power will see this reflected in the academic successes of their students. Although some part of personal power comes from the essential personality of the teacher, it is possible to learn to compensate for areas of weakness and capitalize on areas of strength. Most professional power, however, is based on learned behavior; teachers desiring to improve can recognize and work on those teaching abilities they consider weak.

It is my hope that this book, based on my more than thirty years as a teacher, counsellor, coach, curriculum adviser, and now, university instructor, will serve you as a valuable resource. If you find a few nuggets to prod your personal or professional power, that's good. If you find you are already using ideas, that's even better. Sometimes the reassurance that what you are doing is right, good, and appropriate provides a much-needed nudge to self-confidence and reminds you that you share experiences, concerns, and vulnerabilities with others in your profession. This knowledge can lead to better, more powerful teaching.

Aspects of Personal Power

Caring for Others
Inner Strength
Diligence
Personal Preservation

Aspects of Professional Power

Organization
Teaching Strategies
Communication
Classroom Management
Motivation
Presentation
Leadership

Caring for Others

Everyone knows that teachers care; however, there are times in every teacher's career when caring gets hidden under the piles of work and long lists of responsibilities. At these times, a normally cheerful, compassionate, empathetic, tolerant teacher may appear angry, frustrated, or uninterested. When a teacher's sense of caring diminishes, so does respect—for self, for students, and, in return, *from* students. At these times, you need to "re-work" your personal strengths.

Cheerfulness: If teachers show cheerful faces and attitudes, even if that's not how they are feeling, students will do the same and classes will go more smoothly. People like to be around cheerful people, and teachers who acquire the trait benefit from more energy, good health, serenity, and students with positive attitudes.

Active Compassion: Active compassion is a combination of friendship, loving kindness, understanding, and wisdom that comes from understanding that others "suffer." A compassionate teacher is committed to taking action to better the lot of others and teaches from the heart. The sincere caring for the well-being of others may well be one of the most important qualities of a successful educator.

Empathy: In this fast-paced world of technology, empathy is one powerful trait that teachers have over computers. The showing of genuine, sensitive understanding of the situation of another person, it is necessary to effective teaching. It constitutes the willingness and ability of teachers to put themselves in the shoes of their students and it should always precede the giving of advice.

Tolerance: Tolerance is the ability to see students and peers as they really are and to treat all with respect. It reflects an understanding that stereotyping, scapegoating, or treating anyone unfairly affects the learning, growth, and self-respect of everyone. Tolerance, which helps to establish rapport, enables the teacher to reach and teach all students. It brings a sense of inner peace, more in-class successes, and a greater diversity of student responses.

Respect: Teachers know they should "respect their students if they expect respect in return." But how does one *show* respect? Is it something sensed or demonstrated visibly? We recognize its importance—anyone who has not been given it can tell you—and it behoves us to strive to teach with it. More respect, happiness, personal confidence, and improved student behavior will come to us. Treating others with respect is an indication of caring, and that is what good teaching is all about.

1. Cheerfulness

… from the moment you enter the school in the morning

Have you ever watched a teacher with students and been impressed by the positive energy around her? No doubt, she was smiling.

"OK! I want to know how you do it!" Mrs. Lang said as she burst into her neighbor's classroom one morning.

"Pardon me?" replied her startled colleague, Mrs. Werthmann. "Do what?"

"Make the kids like you! I work just as hard as you. I have good lessons. I use positive reinforcement. I'm just as good a teacher as you, but the kids think you walk on water. They'll do anything for you! How do you do it?"

Mrs. Werthmann shrugged and smiled broadly. "Oh, I'm sure you're exaggerating," she said quietly.

Mrs. Lang sighed, "No! It's true! And it's not fair!" She turned and almost ran into another teacher as she stormed out.

"What's up?" asked Mr. Adams. "Problems? I see Betty's scowling as usual."

"She's just tired," Mrs. Werthmann said and smiled at Mr. Adams. He smiled back and laughed, "See? That's why I like teaching next door to you. You're always smiling and that smile of yours makes me feel better. Now I forget what I came here for but—keep smiling."

Ten Ways to Show Cheerfulness

1. Exercise your face. It takes seventeen muscles to smile, so smile—all the time, at everyone. The worse you are feeling, the more you need to smile. Mark Twain once said that the best way to cheer up is to cheer up somebody else.
2. Practise smiling in a mirror, making sure your eyes and mouth match.
3. Tell yourself you are a cheerful person over and over until it becomes a habit. For example, try the positive affirmation *I am a cheerful person and I like to smile.*
4. Use the "Stop!" technique to avoid cynical or negative thoughts: mentally tell yourself to stop a particular thought if you find something negative creeping in.
5. Strive to make your self-talk, or mental conversations with self, positive, optimistic, and accepting. If you think only of reasons not to be cheerful, it becomes a self-fulfilling prophecy.
6. List activities or situations that make you feel frustrated, angry, or full of some other negative emotion. Choose to avoid these or to approach them with firm resolve to remain as cheerful as possible.
7. Play a tape or CD of a "laugh track," a piece of beautiful music, or a stand-up comedian on the way to work.
8. Remind yourself that you don't have to be happy to be cheerful. Cheerfulness is a deliberate state of mind. Choose to be cheerful. Keep a fresh flower on your desk as a constant reminder of this resolve.
9. Begin every day by doing or saying something to brighten someone else's day. The act of cheering up another person has a wonderful vicarious reaction—it cheers you up too.
10. Slow down. Cheerfulness is lost in the stress of trying to do too much at once. When you find your cheerfulness fading, take a deep breath and walk with exaggerated slowness for about three steps.

2. Active Compassion

… for students, parents, colleagues as well as friends, family, and self

Have you ever noticed that when students are distraught, they often go to one particular teacher in the school? Are you that teacher?

Mrs. May always had the Grade 6 girls in her room—before school, at noon, and after school. In an attempt to find out why, another teacher stood quietly behind the open door to Mrs. May's room during several of these "gatherings." What she discovered was that Mrs. May would stop whatever she was doing, sit quietly, and give her full attention to the girls and their "tales of woe." Then she would offer support and concern. What the interested teacher did not hear was Mrs. May offering solutions to the girls' problems. It seemed that with Mrs. May's guidance, the girls usually figured these out on their own. The teacher was witnessing active compassion. She vowed to improve her own skills in that area.

Ten Ways to Show Active Compassion

1. Provide encouragement all the time. Cultivate positive expectations for others and share these with them.
2. Smile, and mean it, and hug appropriately, then couple this with words of encouragement or positive reinforcement.
3. Be courteous to all your students all the time, and promote courteous behavior in the classroom and school.
4. Do whatever is necessary to make each student feel safe in your room and with you. For example, leave a door open or be careful not to sit too close.
5. Allow your students to take ownership of their learning, that is, involve them in decisions that affect them. Don't be afraid to take a risk by giving them the "power" to make decisions.
6. Cultivate a deep appreciation of others by taking time to get to know them, asking carefully thought-out questions, and listening carefully to their answers. Develop the ability to sense how others are feeling by closely studying body language.
7. Maintain your temper and a calmness of mind even when faced with chaos or an explosive situation.
8. Respect students' friendships. Allow friends to sit together at least some of the time or make positive comments about the friendships.
9. Keep an eye out for anyone who seems to be suffering in any way, perhaps a student looking unhappy or a colleague looking stressed. Try to help, perhaps by being an active listener.
10. Examine all situations, such as playground squabbles or in-class disagreements between peers, as objectively as possible; then make a decision based on the best interests of all.

3. Empathy

… for students, parents, colleagues as well as for friends and family

Have you ever wished you felt less annoyed by and more genuinely concerned about your students or colleagues?

*The eleven-year-old girl left the principal's office in tears. A teacher overheard her explain to a waiting friend: "She doesn't understand. She says she does, but she doesn't. I mean, she answered the phone twice when I was trying to explain. All she said was that it would be OK, and I know it **won't** be OK. How did she get to be principal anyway?"*

Ten Ways to Show Empathy

1. Begin by getting to know your students as individuals so that teacher–student learning is important to them and, if necessary, adapted for them. In this way, your expectations will be aligned with their needs.
2. Treat each student with dignity and respect and expect the same in return.
3. Practise empathetic listening, listening in order to improve the welfare of the speaker. Pay attention to nuances, nonverbal communication, and body language. Consider what is not said. Listen for both words and feelings.
4. Paraphrase content of a conversation and reflect your own feelings.
5. When someone is confiding in you, listen rather than interrupting with "good advice."
6. When listening empathetically to a single student, orient your body to the speaker, maintain eye contact, lean slightly forward, and try to soften your voice when you respond.
7. Ask yourself, *Am I responding in a way that is best for the person?* How you say things is as important as what you say.
8. When talking one-to-one with a student, if unsure about the problem or its underlying causes or confused by the student's words, make an educated guess and proceed, rather than giving up or continually saying, "I don't understand."
9. Treat others as you yourself would like to be treated. This maxim should be the Golden Rule of teaching.
10. Adopt a few empathetic responses that will enable you to respond sincerely and without judgment, at least until you have all the facts. Consider these: "Oh, this is so sad," "Bummer," "That is not good." Also, make noncommittal responses. (*It seems that … It appears to me that …*)

4. Tolerance

… of differences and diversities among students and colleagues

Have you ever wished you could take back words that flew carelessly from your mouth?

The teacher looked around her room in dismay. Students were noisy, out of their desks, off-task. Without thinking, she shouted, "Sit down and be quiet! You're acting like a bunch of wild Indians!"

Immediate silence. Nancy, the lone First Nations student in the room, looked angry and hurt. Her eyes were huge.

The teacher slumped. Oh, if only those awful words spoken in haste …

Ten Ways to Develop Tolerance

1. Practise viewing each student as an individual, with special strengths and weaknesses. Make a three-column chart with headings *Name, Strength,* and *Struggles With,* and fill it in as a constant reminder.
2. Think before you speak. Too often intolerant words are blurted out and cannot be taken back.
3. As a class, create a list of positive things, behaviors, actions, and attitudes that represent tolerance.
4. Coach a sports team and allow *all* students equal time to play regardless of skill.
5. Applaud the opposing team when players do something well.
6. Establish a working relationship with a teacher who is not "just like you." (We tend to favor those who are like us.)
7. Think of how you appear to others. What traits compatible with tolerance do you think they might see in you? Continue to demonstrate these and add to your repertoire, if necessary.
8. Imagine that you have been the victim of identity theft. How would you feel? What would you do? Consider that this is how someone treated with intolerance feels.
9. Start a school club that deals with diversity. Invite students from as many different backgrounds, cultures, and races as possible, then discuss areas of concern, if there are any, potential problems faced by diverse populations, possible solutions, and commonalities.
10. If you have an opportunity, learn as much as you can about a family of a different culture/nationality, with which you are unfamiliar, in an attempt to increase personal knowledge and awareness. Be sure to share aspects of your own background.

5. Respect

… for your students, your career, and yourself

Have you ever silently envied the obvious respect that a colleague received from students?

"Mr. Ladd is the best," Sheila said with confidence.
   "Why?" asked her mother.
   "He never yells. He talks real calm and looks right at you even when he's mad."
   "Does he get mad often?"
   "Oh, sometimes, when the boys do dumb stuff. But he still talks real soft." Sheila smiled. "He treats us with respect."
   "Oh," her mother murmured, amazed that her six-year-old daughter understood the concept. She silently vowed to thank Mr. Ladd the next time they met.

Ten Ways to Show Respect

1. Treat students and colleagues with consideration and high regard. Doing this means taking the time to get to know them. Find out their likes, dislikes, concerns, and worries. Remember that respect begets respect.
2. Maintain eye contact and try to be on the same level as the student when talking one-to-one. If this means squatting down beside his desk, or sitting her on a bigger chair, then so be it.
3. Dress appropriately. It shows respect if you take the time to "look professional."
4. Avoid coffee-breath (or any other bad breath), to deal with one of students' pet peeves with teachers. Carry breath mints.
5. Listen actively to what students say. If you don't have time to listen, say so, and set a time when you can.
6. Deal with inappropriate behaviors one-on-one to avoid student embarrassment.
7. Always behave politely in the classroom and staff room. Never shout.
8. In conversation, focus on the positive points of students and colleagues, as well as of your school.
9. If you make a mistake, accept this as an example of growth and never put yourself down. In this way, you respect yourself and set a good example.
10. Diligently support school codes, rules, and regulations to show respect for your school.

Inner Strength

Teachers need more than their share of inner strength: the clear life direction that provides the confidence, serenity, and patience to control harmful or unnecessary impulses and to take constructive action. Inner strength is really will power at work. It keeps us in our profession, even though the "perks" or rewards often seem few and far between. Those of us that love what we do are the most able to motivate students and do our jobs well—we have inner strength. We are assertive, self-confident, socially competent, persevering, and peaceful within ourselves.

Assertiveness: Teachers need to balance empathy with assertiveness. Students in the class of an assertive teacher know the boundaries and expectations; as a result, they are more focused and involved. Colleagues treat assertive teachers with more respect and are less likely to delegate unnecessarily. Assertiveness also breeds confidence.

Self-Confidence: Every teacher knows the feeling of butterflies in the stomach at the beginning of a school year and bouts of uncertainty in the months to come. That is normal. Truly self-confident teachers, though, suffer fewer of these doubts and stresses: they play to their strengths while working to overcome weakness. Their self-confidence radiates to those around them. It leads to academic successes for students and more poise for the teachers.

Self-Esteem: Self-esteem differs from self-confidence in that it is more connected to an overall opinion of how we value our character and capabilities. It usually precedes self-confidence. The power of self-esteem lies in how it affects the ability to teach. If, for example, you *feel* you are a good teacher, you will probably *be* a good teacher. Although teaching is an influential, necessary, and worthy profession, the self-esteem of many teachers is often less than it should be for optimal success. Developing positive self-esteem will strengthen personal feelings of energy, peacefulness, optimism, and potential for teaching well and influencing others.

Social Competence: More than "being friendly," social competence is a condition of positive regard that speaks to what we are as social beings living in groups and caring for others. A socially competent teacher interacts well with students, experiencing more happiness, as well as openness from others, and serving as a great role model for social behavior in students.

Perseverance: We have been inundated with catchy phrases such as "Perseverance is the key" and "Perseverance pays off," and as teachers, we agree. We are also aware that perseverance is not obstinacy or stubbornness. As Henry Ward Beecher put it, "The difference between perseverance and obstinacy is that one often comes from a strong will, and the other from a strong won't." Perseverance is a commitment to complete a challenge as well as possible, a necessary trait for success in teaching. Exercising it brings self-confidence and satisfaction in meeting goals.

Peacefulness: This state of serenity and tranquility allows the teacher to deal with issues calmly and justly. Peaceful teachers make the best facilitators, instructors, and counsellors—hence, the best teachers. They are also excellent models for nonviolent behavior, subject to less stress, frustration, and anger. Peacefulness is one of the most powerful personal traits a teacher can have; without it, the daily maelstrom of activity in the classroom, together with the myriad demands on a teacher's time, can easily lead to mental distress or physical illness.

6. Assertiveness

… when dealing with students and colleagues no matter where

Have you ever found yourself saying, "Yes, OK, I'll do it," when you know that taking on that task may well be the last straw for you? Similarly, have you ever "given in" to students' whines and complaints and removed a consequence you vowed would stand strong?

"Please, Ms. Lee, just another few days for our reports," Josh begged. "I've been so busy with all the piles of homework, and hockey, and …"

"OK, OK," Ms. Lee sighed. "Two more days." This was the third time she'd allowed her fifth graders to talk her into a delay on this assignment. She wondered if she was helping them or simply avoiding a confrontation.

She didn't see Josh give his friend a high five in the hall, or hear him chuckle, "See, I told ya she'd back down again. No sweat!"

Ten Ways to Show Assertiveness

1. Set clear, reasonable classroom goals, limits, and guidelines and expect student compliance.
2. React quickly and with calm confidence in any situations requiring behavioral management. Use statements such as *I need you to …* Speak clearly and maintain eye contact.
3. Before reacting, listen carefully to all requests or suggestions. Think time often precludes inappropriate responses.
4. Adopt a warm, genuinely caring attitude toward students and peers.
5. Request and expect help (from peers, parents, specialists, and students) when you need it, and learn to say "no."
6. Provide clear, concise directions for tasks, activities, assignments, and expectations, leaving no room for miscommunication. (See "Providing Clear Directions," page 55.)
7. Carefully plan both short- and long-term goals and objectives for students and for yourself so you know where you are going.
8. Observe your personal rights as well as the rights of your students. Create wall charts listing them.
9. Establish realistic consequences and adhere to them consistently.
10. Understand your own importance and stick to your word, whether you are being asked for an extension from students, bombarded with possibly unrealistic requests from parents, or begged by peers to take on extra, unwanted responsibilities.

7. Self-Confidence

… to be the excellent teacher you truly are

Have you ever felt you weren't good enough at your job? That you just didn't have what it takes?

Nobody wanted to coach the girls' volleyball team. It was a lot of work—especially since the team had not won a game for ages. Miss Always finally agreed to take on the job. A five-foot, ninety-pound woman, she knew nothing about volleyball, but she had confidence. When she first spoke to the unhappy-looking team, she said, "This is wonderful! I've never won a volleyball championship and so this will be my first. I can hardly wait to get started!" The strange part was the girls believed her and that year they nearly did win the championship.

Ten Ways to Develop Self-Confidence

1. Make a list of all your strengths and weaknesses. Capitalize on the former by playing to them whenever possible. For example, if good at art, offer to do bulletin boards. Address your weak areas.
2. List ten things-to-do you only "tolerate." Begin eliminating them, delegating them, or altering them in some way.
3. Maintain good health by sleeping, eating, and exercising properly. Drink lots of water daily and keep a bottle on your desk. Physical confidence precedes mental confidence.
4. Maintain excellent posture. (Imagine a thread attaching your head to the ceiling.) It makes you feel and look confident.
5. Aim to keep a positive attitude; refuse to accept undue criticism, even from yourself.
6. In a potentially self-conscious situation, focus on an object, such as a plant, and consider it in detail (shape, function, color, texture).
7. Ask for what you want. You may not get it, but asking for it will improve the odds.
8. Practise "feel-good" thoughts. When your confidence is lagging, think of things, places, or people that make you feel good.
9. Use physical relaxation techniques throughout the day. Relax your neck, shoulders, and so on. Imagine that your body is composed of a silky liquid. Visualize and "feel" a smooth flow of warmth rising from your feet to the top of your head.
10. Play the I Am game. Ask yourself how a confident person would behave in a situation, then say, "I am confident in …" Emulate those behaviors.

8. Self-Esteem

… in teaching and in life generally

Why is it that some teachers radiate an aura of high self-esteem and worth? Have you ever wondered if they had a secret you'd like to know?

The members of a hiring committee debated long and hard over two potentially excellent candidates for a position. The scales were tipped, however, when the principal asked quietly, "Which of the two appears to have a greater sense of self-esteem?" When we thought about this, some obvious traits came to mind and we knew exactly which candidate would have the most success dealing with the difficult Grade 6 class.

Ten Ways to Strengthen Self-Esteem

1. Celebrate your own accomplishments, and take credit for your successes. Avoid mistaking this as false pride—it is awareness of self.
2. Acknowledge a wrong or mistake you have committed, learn to forgive yourself, and realize you are nonetheless the same worthwhile person. To help with this, ask yourself, *If my friend did this, would I forgive him?*
3. Remind yourself that human variety and uniqueness are necessary and worthwhile, and believe in the basic worth of *every* human being.
4. Set goals that can be reached. Avoid setting personal standards higher and higher. Neither overachievement nor underachievement contributes to self-worth.
5. Learn to like yourself unconditionally. This means liking yourself no matter who or what you are, or what you have or have not done.
6. Remember to be kind to yourself. Responsibility is taking care of yourself first so that you can offer care to others. A burned-out teacher helps no one.
7. Remind yourself that happiness is not dependent on career success.
8. List everything you have gained from others, such as knowledge, awareness, understandings, and even personality traits. Then ask yourself, *If I was not worthwhile, would they have bothered?*
9. Remember that you are the star of your own life. Pretend you are viewing a movie about yourself. As the star, you must be a worthwhile person.
10. Avoid "shoulding." Beginning thoughts or sentences with "I should have ..." reduces self-esteem. *Should*s are value judgments and are better replaced with such openings as "I want ...," "I prefer ...," or "I did ..."

9. Social Competence

… in relation to people around you in school and in life

Think back to your school years. Was there a teacher with whom you had great rapport? Chances are that teacher displayed a high degree of social competence.

"Dad, you look upset," the eight-year-old said, calmly putting an arm around her seated father. "Want to talk about it?"

The father raised his eyes. Was this his little daughter being so perceptive and caring? "I do feel down. Had a tough day today," he found himself replying.

"Well, you need a hug," the girl said confidentially and wrapped her arms around her father.

"Where did you learn to talk like that?" he asked as he hugged her back.

"Teacher—at school," the child replied.

"Hmmm," said the father, and realized that suddenly he did feel better.

Ten Ways to Display Social Competence

1. Model the appropriate expression of negative emotions. Teach students skills for coping with these emotions and the stressors they face daily.
2. Consistently reinforce positive behavior. Model this and teach students to reinforce one another. Encourage students to practise giving positive feedback to others, even if the situation is explosive or sensitive. Model for them how to follow these interactions with a discussion wherein the students describe, as truthfully and accurately as possible, what they saw occur and what they contributed.
3. Ask open-ended questions about students' emotional status, and listen actively to the responses.
4. Greet students and peers with sincere compassion and respect. Present yourself with a smile, relaxed, "open" body position, and easy-to-talk-to manner.
5. When conflict arises, paraphrase or restate what you believe you heard. In this way, you will be focusing on the truth rather than on a misconception.
6. When speaking to students and colleagues, be sure to use their names.
7. Present thoughts and opinions in a polite way, without sounding arrogant or egotistical. Keep an open mind, which indicates your willingness to accept the ideas of others, too.
8. Own your own decisions, mistakes, and shortcomings—avoid blaming others.
9. Be aware of what you are saying nonverbally. Is your manner open and inviting? Do your eyes match your voice? Students are quick to pick up discrepancies.
10. Describe all behavior—even problem behavior—in positive terms. For example, say, *What you should do …* rather than *What you shouldn't do …*

10. Perseverance

… when faced with challenges posed by the curriculum, student behaviors, and professional duties

Mrs. Dillon was perplexed. She had tried everything she could think of to teach long division to Gary, but without success. As a rule, she was not one to give up easily, but this time she was getting nowhere. Both teacher and student were frustrated. It seemed they both assumed failure was unavoidable. That was until a familiar TV commercial caught Mrs. Dillon's attention: "Buy now, pay later." That was it! Mrs. Dillon knew what she had to do. The next day she informed Gary they would put aside long division for the next few weeks. His demeanour visibly lightened and a weight was instantly lifted from the teacher's shoulders. Three weeks later, they tackled the challenge again—this time with success.

Ten Ways to Practise Perseverance

1. Break challenges into small, manageable chunks and work on single chunks at a time.
2. Reward yourself after completing small steps in the challenge—don't wait for the end accomplishment. For example, promise yourself a favorite coffee after school.
3. Persevere enthusiastically. Positive enthusiasm makes difficult steps seem easier.
4. Attempt to determine possible roadblocks before undertaking a challenge, and have a few strategies for overcoming these on hand.
5. Remind yourself that the ability to persevere is a measure of self-control and that you are in charge.
6. Avoid accepting challenges that you *know* you will not be able to master or complete.
7. Adopt the "Yes-Know" philosophy when you and the students face a challenge. Say to them, "*Yes*, this will be tough, but you *know* how to learn and I *know* how to teach. Together, we'll make it." You will find that this has a positive effect.
8. Allow yourself a time-out when faced with a seemingly insurmountable roadblock. Avoid everything to do with the challenge, even thinking about it, for at least 48 hours. Then retackle it with enthusiasm.
9. Keep a running record of the minutes spent on a daunting challenge. If the hours add up without success, it may be time to consider alternatives.
10. Remind yourself that sometimes it is OK to admit defeat. If you have truly persevered, you have not shown weakness.

11. Peacefulness

… of spirit and soul

Have you ever watched the behavior of a great mentor and wished that you projected the same sense of inner peace?

"Boy, that class was loud. I have a headache," the teacher complained to a colleague.

"Not very peaceful, hey?" replied the peer.

"Peaceful? You gotta be kidding. They were on a war path."

"So what did you do?"

"I just yelled louder than they did until they heard me."

"Did that help?"

The distraught teacher sighed. "No," she murmured.

The peer just smiled slightly and nodded, "We need to be peace models," she added quietly, "every minute of the day."

Ten Ways to Promote Feeling Peaceful

1. Before getting out of bed in the morning, relax, take three deep breaths, stretch fully, and create a peaceful feeling in your heart. Aim to start the day in a positive mood.

2. Create a personal affirmation and repeat it to yourself throughout the day. You might say, *I am strong and today I will be more patient* or *I am compassionate and today I will …*

3. Practise awareness on the way to work. Look carefully at little details, like a bird on a wire, snow on a lawn, raindrops running down the windshield.

4. Draw a lifeline, and be aware of where you are now, how far you have come, and where you would like to be in the future. Such a visible indicator often provides a sense of inner calm, a positive reminder of growth and accomplishments, and a visual image of the future.

5. Identify things, situations, or people causing you stress. Find constructive ways to overcome these stresses or apply stress management techniques. (See "Tension Taming Techniques," next page.)

6. If, for example, you find that you have taken on an extracurricular expectation requiring more time than budgeted for or if you are faced with inappropriately angry parents in a conference, try to disengage as quickly as possible. Accepting an early defeat is easier than a final one.

7. Accept that you cannot be all things to all people and that at times you will fail.

8. Practise forgiveness. Forgive any person who has hurt you in any way. You will thereby release anger, which is detrimental to feeling peaceful.

9. If possible, avoid any situation where you know you will feel threatened—feeling threatened makes one defensive. If you cannot avoid the situation, find a way to lessen your involvement.

10. Exercise, especially through yoga or classes focusing on stretching, and remember the benefit of a long walk outside.

Tension Taming Techniques

- Learn to recognize the things, people, and situations that cause you stress, as well as your personal signals of stress, such as a headache or quickness of breath.

- List the moments of happiness, peace, and joy you have had in the past week. If these are few, you may have reached your stress quota. Insist on taking a time-out; one of the best ways to do this is to go for a long walk.

- Stand apart from trivial classroom conflicts, such as the "he-did-it-first" or "she-took-my …" arguments, or from unimportant disagreements that arise in the staff room, such as who cleans the microwave. Choose your battles carefully. Avoid the ones where failure is probable unless this avoidance would lead to personal reproach for not having fought at all. Consider each situation separately.

- Consider yourself a "teacher in progress" as opposed to a "teacher product." Accept that you are always growing and learning and are allowed mistakes.

- Do a personal quick-check by asking, *If I had only one month to live, what would I do differently?* Then, if possible, do it, or at least something close to it.

- Get enough rest. Plan for two hours rest more than usual at least once a week. If you have trouble sleeping, try meditating, listening to relaxation music, using guided imagery (tell yourself a story), or discussing the matter with a doctor.

- Practise mind games when you are forced to wait. For example: Count the ceiling tiles; make mental lists of things to do; review the words to a familiar song.

- Look at the beauty around you. Make a point of finding one miracle a day, perhaps something as simple as snow sparkling in the sun.

- Take up a hobby and put aside a fixed amount of time for it weekly.

- Take at least part of every day and weekend to do something totally unrelated to school. Push all thoughts of work from your mind.

- Avoid negative coping patterns such as substance abuse, overwork, and eating dysfunctions. If these are present and you cannot remove them yourself, seek professional help.

- Carefully assess whether you are caught in any stress-promoting life traps (see following section). If you suffer from any of these, it may be time to seek professional counsel.

Stress-Promoting Life Traps

- **Indispensability Syndrome:** If you suffer from this, remove the idea from your mind. No one is indispensable. Think of a teacher who has had to take a long period away from school. In most cases, the class survived perfectly in her absence.
- **Workaholism:** Teachers are often workaholics—they work long hours and wear themselves out. Remember the proverb about "all work and no play." Remember also that the more fatigued you are, the less likely you are to teach well and the more likely you are to get ill.
- **Success Addiction:** Our culture admires successful people, yet teaching seldom seems to be viewed as an admired or esteemed profession. Possibly to overcome this societal oversight, teachers may feel driven to work faster and harder all the time—a sure stress trap. It is better to remind ourselves that spending quality time with the students is more important than spreading ourselves so thin that no one benefits.
- **Multi-tasking Nightmare:** If you find you are doing too many things, moving too quickly, seldom completing anything well, then you may be suffering from this stress promoter. It's time to take stock—and make choices. Research has shown that tasks completed by a "multi-tasker" are often not finished as well as the same tasks done by someone who spends more time and focus on the activity.
- **Type A Personality:** Many teachers are Type A personalities: driven to be excessively competitive, impatient, and often suffering from a sense of urgency. They can even be overly assertive, even aggressive, with others who interfere with their forward rush of activity. If you recognize this about yourself, realize the inherent stress traps.
- **Insecurity:** *Has it been worth it? Am I good enough?* Teachers who constantly self-question and second-guess themselves like this may be heading for a stress breakdown. It may be better to focus only on "positive completions" in order to break a cycle of doubt.
- **Superman Complex:** The teachers who take on more and more responsibility with the belief they will never break down are jumping head first into a stress trap. Know your personal limits; if you are unaware of them, listen to friends, family members, or peers who are usually quick to comment on them.
- **Not-My-Fault Syndrome:** The teachers who constantly view students functioning below expectations as "not their fault" are playing a blame game that can lead to feelings of guilt and stress. It is good to remember that when a student fails, a teacher fails even more.
- **Poor-Me Syndrome:** "My job is too tough." "I don't get paid enough for all this stress." Teachers who constantly complain about their jobs or feel sorry for themselves are heading toward stress breakdowns. If the job is not for you, perhaps you are wise to consider a change.
- **Reinventing-the-Wheel Addiction:** Teachers who believe that only the material they create is good enough for their students constantly "create" new worksheets, tasks, activities, or units. They are in a sure stress trap. With ample excellent resources available, there is no need to constantly originate materials.
- **The Wendy Syndrome:** Based on *Peter Pan*'s Wendy, who mothered all the Lost Boys, this syndrome concerns teachers who mistakenly feel they can help everyone all the time. The stress of trying to live up to these unrealistic expectations can build quickly.

Diligence

When we consider what is at stake—the future of our youth—it becomes essential that teachers are conscientious, meticulous, well informed, and reliable. We know we must be consistently observant—attentive to the smallest of details—competent, knowledgeable, and, above all, dependable. Our professional integrity depends on being powerful in all these areas and in taking delight in our roles.

Attention to Detail: As teachers, we know that the ability to observe what is going on outside ourselves is essential. Of equal importance is the ability to pay attention to an inner voice, to value intuition. In order to teach with power, teachers need to see what is present and to consider what is not. The observant teacher enjoys more creativity and confidence, wastes less time and energy, and experiences less frustration.

Professional Competence: This strength means being knowledgeable about the curriculum and strategies for implementing it, but also about children, their individual learning styles, growth patterns, wants, and needs. Achieving competence is a tall order, but results in more success with students, a sense of personal security, and confidence. "Winging it" is minimized.

Active Learning and Professional Growth: As far as students are concerned, teachers are expected to know *everything*. As unrealistic as this may seem, there is truth to it. In order to teach powerfully, we need to know about such things as child development, learning styles, and curriculum materials; we also need to keep up with change and to have some personal time. Balancing these needs permits teachers to enjoy more student respect and self-confidence.

Dependability: Dependability is closely connected to honesty and trustworthiness. It means you can be counted on to keep your word and offer support to the best of your ability. All teachers will instantly recognize that this trait is essential to the development of rapport with students and, consequently, to successful teaching. The dependable teacher, a true mentor to students, will help to create mutual respect and cohesiveness in the classroom. This teacher enjoys inner peace, respect from and for students, and student confidence in the information shared and taught and in the teacher as confidant.

Integrity: Integrity is a complicated mix of morals and virtues. The teacher who teaches with integrity teaches from the heart, connecting with the students and turning them on to learning as well as to the love of learning. This powerful teacher lives in harmony with self and is truly happy with the career choice made.

12. Attention to Detail

… in the daily classroom routine

Have you ever missed something a student did, such as forming a cursive letter correctly, that was slightly different or "better" than what he had done in the past?

The class was moving along smoothly when all of a sudden a person wearing a ski mask dashed in, swiped the teacher's purse from her desk, and ran out.

Noticeably unperturbed, the teacher smiled and said, "Now, who can tell me what my purse looked like? It has been on my desk since the first day of school." There were a few random guesses, but no details volunteered.

"OK," the teacher continued, "describe the vandal." Descriptions varied and were scant and mostly incorrect.

"Now," said the teacher, "what have we learned?"

Ten Ways to Pay Attention to Detail

1. Take the "How Observant Are You?" quiz (next page) for a quick check on your attention to detail. If you score less than half of them right, make a deliberate effort to pay more attention to your surroundings. (*Note:* The questions from 11 to 18 should have particular relevance to teachers.)

2. Consciously take every opportunity to look for details. (For example: When waiting for a traffic light, check car models or licence plates; count how many houses are on a particular street; look closely at people's nonverbal communication.)

3. Pay attention to facts. Keep anecdotal notes on everything; organize these weekly, summarizing what you need to keep and discarding the rest.

4. Allow yourself time, perhaps an hour a week during a quiet walk, to consider the implications and possibilities of current situations. It takes time to develop introspective abilities. Be patient.

5. When you receive facts from observation, ask yourself questions about them. (*How can I … What do I …*) You thereby use both sides of your brain.

6. Pay attention to what your students or colleagues are wearing on a particular day. Try to recall these details that evening. Little trials like this improve observation skills.

7. Act on your first impressions or ideas about facts you receive. If you have observed the facts skeptically, intuition is right more often than wrong.

8. Strive to "be in the moment," to pay attention to what is happening right around you.

9. Learn to meditate or at least to allow yourself quiet think-and-reflect time on a regular basis.

10. Avoid multi-tasking if possible. This approach, although sometimes necessary, does not allow for careful observation.

How Observant Are You?

1. Try to recall what the school secretary was wearing yesterday.
2. What did you (or your family) have for dinner last Sunday?
3. Try to recall any small details of a TV program you recently watched.
4. On the standard traffic light, is the red at the top or the bottom?
5. What two signs are found on a telephone number pad?
6. Describe the standard Yield sign.
7. What is the difference between the top and bottom sides of a standard floppy disc?
8. What images are on the back of the most recent Canadian five-dollar bill?
9. On a No pedestrians road sign, which way is the walking figure facing?
10. Describe the logo of your favorite channel (situated in the bottom right-hand corner of the screen), recording studio, or food-producing company (e.g., Quaker).
11. Describe the logo of your school board.
12. Visualize the main doors to your school. What color and size are they? What do the door handles look like?
13. Visualize the school playground. Mentally describe the equipment. What are the colors? shapes? designs?
14. Describe your school letterhead.
15. Visualize your class. Mentally move from student to student and describe how each holds a pencil.
16. Visualize your class when students are reading silently or being read to and focus on how each student sits (or fidgets).
17. Visualize your class during a writing assignment. Do certain students assume the same postures all the time?
18. Recall a favorite picture book you share with your students. Describe the first visual image or illustration in the book.

You will be your own judge as to how well you observe. What we look at closely is determined at least in part by our personal interests. Since we are teachers, the final eight responses should be relatively easy. You may be surprised at how often you look at something, but don't really see it.

Answers

1–3: Responses will vary.
4. top
5. #, *
6. Inverted triangle, red rim, silver interior
7. Bottom has a metal circle in the centre.
8. Children skating, tobogganing and playing hockey
9. The pedestrian always faces toward the road
10–18: Responses will vary.

13. Professional Competence

... as an educator

How often have you had to "fake" your way through a lesson, or rely completely on what was in a teachers' manual, because you lacked the knowledge or facts necessary to instruct well?

"What are you going to do this weekend?" Melissa asked her Grade 4 teacher.

"Well, actually, I'm going to go to school."

"You mean here?"

"No. I'm really going to school. To a class. To learn. It's at a meeting hall downtown," the teacher said, smiling.

"No way! You mean teachers go to school too?"

"Yes," the teacher laughed, "and we go to Safeway, Sears, and pretty much all the places you go."

"Cool!" Melissa bounced off and the teacher smiled, hoping she had helped to dispel a common teacher myth.

Ten Ways to Strengthen Professional Competence

1. Always be well prepared. Students deserve no less. Find a planning procedure that works for you and use it faithfully.
2. Keep on your desk a few well-chosen books or binders for quick referral for things such as grammar how-to, fill-in activities, and lists of activities related to specific subjects.
3. Regularly read a newspaper or watch the news. Often busy teachers opt out of this responsibility to do marking or planning.
4. Subscribe to an educational journal and read it during silent reading at school.
5. Rather than Web surfing for answers to specific questions, invite a few students to do this for you. This is efficient use of time for you, a learning situation for them.
6. List your shortcomings as a teacher—ask your students to help if you can't think of any—then work at overcoming these, one at a time.
7. If you have not already done so, write out your philosophy of education, ensuring that it includes personal goals. Periodically consider whether it has changed and check your progress.
8. Ask yourself how much you really care about the growth of your students and how committed you are to their learning. If you suspect this is an area of personal weakness, talk to a friend, colleague, or mentor and find a way to overcome it. (For example: Teach a different grade or course, or take some time off.)
9. Realize the importance of all students' values and ideas by encouraging students to recognize and discuss these regularly.
10. Read everything you can about teaching and children. Be curious!

14. Active Learning and Professional Growth

… about the curriculum, the students, and the specific subject matter

How often have you had to "pretend" you knew something about which you actually knew nothing?

"I don't know the answer to that question," Ms. Wallis said.

"You always say you don't know," complained a student. *"Why don't you know? You're the teacher."*

Ms. Wallis swallowed. She had been saying that a lot lately. But it wasn't her fault she got stuck teaching Grade 5 Science. She wasn't a Science major. Then a little voice nagged in her head. "You're the teacher. It's your job to know!"

That weekend Ms. Wallis enrolled in a Science workshop at which she asked numerous questions not only of the instructor, but of colleagues who also taught the subject. When she arrived at school on Monday, she felt a great weight lifted off her shoulders.

Ten Ways to Grow Professionally

1. Exchange units or lessons on different themes or subjects with a colleague.
2. Ask the school librarian to put the latest information about curriculum or resources into your mailbox on a loan basis.
3. Initiate a Knowledge Sharing group with one or two colleagues, where you meet weekly for half an hour to share latest findings related to curriculum, effective teaching strategies, specific course content, and so on.
4. Take a course (not necessarily directly related to teaching) once every other year. If you are reluctant to do this on your own, convince a colleague to register with you. You will both benefit.
5. At a convention, be sure to attend sessions in areas of your personal weakness, rather than because a speaker is funny or entertaining.
6. Work an exchange with a peer teacher whereby you observe her for a day and she observes you for a day. (Usually, a principal will provide coverage for personal development such as this.) Provide each other with constructive criticism.
7. Ask to be evaluated regularly, either by the principal or other person in authority, and expect and accept graciously the feedback.
8. Invest in your own development. Take advantage of every possible professional development opportunity offered by your school board or institution. Learning is forever, curriculum keeps changing, and talking with your peers is advantageous.
9. At least once yearly, make time to attend available workshops that are not directly connected to the school (e.g., a class on meditation, a workshop on painting).
10. Ask good questions of peers, experts, or other professionals, and write the responses in a log or journal.

15. Dependability

... as related to honesty and trustworthiness

How often have you had that nagging feeling that you haven't done something you were supposed to do? And you are a dependable person—aren't you?

Letter from a Grade 3 student:

I love Mrs. Skellig. She always does what she says she'll do and she tells the truth. Not like some teachers who just pretend a lot. I can tell her stuff and it's OK. She doesn't tell the other teachers or kids. I love Mrs. Skellig.
Signed,
Nancy W

Ten Ways to Show Dependability

1. Make every attempt to keep promises. Avoid making promises or setting consequences you cannot keep. If you have inadvertently gotten into this awkward position, admit your personal mistake or failure, apologize, and accept the consequences.
2. Keep the conditions and lines of demarcation between students and teacher clear so that everyone knows these and will not, therefore, face unpleasant surprises. Students should know exactly what the teacher will and will not do.
3. Meet deadlines, whether from your principal, school district, or yourself. It is your professional responsibility to do so.
4. Maintain accurate, up-to-date records. It is a good idea to keep individual folders for each student.
5. Arrive at school on time (or early) and always be prepared. Have your plans organized, your head in "teaching zone," and your smile ready.
6. Provide parents with honest, not sugar-coated reports. They need to trust that the information you give them about their child is accurate.
7. If you are unable to provide certain, perhaps sensitive information to students, tell them ahead of time.
8. Work with thoroughness, a part of dependability. Do the best you can with what you have.
9. Accept only those responsibilities you can meet. Learn to say "no" and to delegate.
10. When you are late meeting a responsibility (it will happen), avoid making excuses. Accept responsibility, offer apologies, and promise to complete the project as soon as possible.

16. Integrity

… in the role of educator

Can you remember a teacher from your youth who stood out from the rest? Most probably, that teacher taught with integrity.

I had a teacher who exemplified the saying "to thine own self be true." He not only kept all of us captivated by his every word, he also was quick to take a stand in defence of his beliefs. When a particularly sensitive topic arose in our high school discussion class, he paused for a moment and then deliberately allowed us to pursue the subject at length. When confronted by authorities on this decision, he simply said, "It was in the best interests of all."

Ten Ways to Practise Integrity

1. Know yourself. Make a list of your personal and professional goals, in hierarchical order, so that you know what is important to you. Write them into your philosophy of education.
2. Act deliberately on important issues, prepared to take a stand for what you believe in.
3. When faced with a conflict, take time to consider several possible solutions and their effects on both yourself and others. You will want to make the choice that best aligns with your personal philosophy and value system. Acting on impulse may jeopardize your integrity as a teacher.
4. Hold true to your commitments. Know what is expected of you and then do it in the time allowed.
5. Make only promises (or consequences) you can keep and endeavour to see all projects through to the end.
6. Teach in a way that reflects who you are, what your interests and beliefs are, and what your vulnerabilities are.
7. Show intellectual responsibility. Keep up-to-date with your field by attending conferences and workshops.
8. Practise this age-old dictum: If you can't say something nice, don't say anything at all.
9. Respect your students by taking a private, one-on-one approach if you want to discuss issues personal to them. Tell them honestly what you think. (*I suspect you are …*)
10. Commit yourself to being the best teacher you can be, one who enjoys the job without ambivalence toward its demands.

Personal Preservation

Not caring for themselves as well as they care for their students is the downfall of many teachers. When it comes to taking care of their physical and mental health, teachers sometimes put themselves "at the bottom of the list." They fail to give themselves the time they need to recharge as effective, influential educators. In order to teach well and influence children, teachers must maintain optimum health and wellness—teaching excellence is lost when the teacher loses sleep, health, mental acuity, or sense of self. Teachers also need the support and guidance offered by a mentor and once in a while the challenge and opportunities offered by a major professional change.

Sustainable Energy: Many factors contribute to teacher burnout, a significant problem presenting itself as an overall condition of fatigue. (To determine if you are at the danger level for burnout, do the "Are You Burning Out?" quiz, page 34.) Teachers always seem to overexert themselves, making them good candidates for this debilitating state. Knowing how to sustain productive energy enables them to maintain more serenity and avoid burnout.

Wisdom of Having a Mentor: In a relationship built on trust, a mentor provides a sounding board for ideas, frustrations, fears, and accomplishments. This person helps with the resetting of goals, if they are unobtainable, or to celebrate the ones reached. A mentor also helps with the re-evaluation of strength and teaching power, and can provide encouragement to slow down when overexertion is imminent. All teachers benefit from having a mentor, often, but not always, a close personal friend.

Courage to Change: Teachers, if they are to maintain optimum power, need regular changes in their procedures, courses, grades, or schools. Change is good. It can be as insignificant as making upgrades to existing materials, or as big as changing schools. The latter, although fraught with anxiety for many, is a sure-fire way to stimulate personal growth and increase teaching power.

17. Sustainable Energy

… or knowing how to prevent burnout to teach as long as you want to

Have you ever felt as if you lacked the energy or desire to teach one more student, one more day?

Everyone was surprised when Mrs. Nolan didn't show up for work one day and no substitute appeared to take her class. It was several days before the truth became known. Mrs. Nolan, exhausted and sick, had been hospitalized with pneumonia and total exhaustion. Her peers' surprise turned to shock. How had that happened? Had there been warning signs of burnout? Then one teacher recalled that Mrs. Nolan had volunteered for a third extracurricular activity that term. Another noted that she had provided tutorials almost every night and that she was always the first to arrive in the morning and the last to leave at night. There were other indicators too. Mrs. Nolan often spent entire weekends working on a curriculum committee. And with her many talents, she was usually the first person approached when someone needed help with anything artistic. The other teachers were silent. "Burnout" had been written all over their peer and none of them had even noticed.

Ten Ways to Sustain Energy and Prevent Burnout

1. Check your humor content regularly. If you find you are laughing *at* students or colleagues rather than *with* them, reduce stressful situations and refocus your humor by checking to see that you do not laugh at others. Budget laugh time into every day. (Refer to "Teaching with a Sense of Humor," page 72, for good ideas.)
2. Recognize, and list, your limitations; refuse to engage in an activity that focuses on an area of weakness. No one can be everything to everyone.
3. Create self-time, even if it means something is left undone. Allow yourself at least thirty minutes a day and longer on weekends—a necessary preventative measure.
4. Examine your personal self-talk. Is it negative? If so, play the Stop game, where you tell yourself to stop any unconstructive thoughts, shift to positive thoughts, and take stress reduction measures. (See "Tension Taming Techniques," page 23.)
5. Find something you enjoy—a hobby, reading, movies, music—and *make* time for it regularly. Understand that you are not being selfish, but if you allow yourself to burn out, you are.
6. Learn how to behave assertively and to avoid feelings of guilt. (See Assertiveness, page 17.)
7. Spend some time with active, joyful people *not* in the teaching profession.
8. Establish a strong, social support group of people with similar likes, hobbies, traits, and interests and meet with them regularly. They need not be other teachers.
9. Practise self-reinforcement. (See "Self-Reinforcement Strategies, page 35.")
10. Get a pet (even a goldfish is enough). The responsibility inherent in pet ownership has a positive effect on energy. For example, taking a dog for a walk when feeling overwhelmed by so much to do will boost your overall energy.

Are You Burning Out?

If you answer "Yes" to more than half of these questions, take steps to reduce burnout risk.

- Do you dread Mondays?

- Are you too tired to spend quality time with family or friends?

- Do you suffer from insomnia or eating disorders?

- Are you snapping at others or jumping to overly quick conclusions?

- Do you regularly give up personal time to catch up on work-related items?

- Are you always tired?

- Are you often "slightly sick" with colds, coughs, or sore throat, but not sick enough to stay home?

- Do you suffer from frequent headaches?

- Has your usual sense of humor disappeared or waned?

- Do you seem to be getting further and further behind no matter how hard you work?

- Are you resorting to more "winging it" and less solid, productive planning?

- Do colleagues or friends ask you frequently if you are feeling OK?

- Have you lost or gained weight unexplainably?

- Do you wake up very early, around 3 a.m., and find your mind racing so that you are unable to return to sleep?

- Is your desk piling up with papers that you don't seem to have time to deal with?

- Have you noticed your students becoming less positive in class, perhaps as a result of your "less positive" approach?

- Do you find yourself avoiding previously enjoyed activities, such as eating lunch in the staff room or going for coffee with friend?

Self-Reinforcement Strategies

- At the end of each day, recall a positive moment. Even on the worst days, one moment will be worth remembering.

- Record all your successes. Refer to this Success Journal when you are feeling down.

- Focus on areas of improvement in the class and share these with the students. The good thing can be something very small, such as all students remembering to write the date on a worksheet.

- Consider the end of the workday as the beginning of a "new day," the time that belongs to you and your family. Choose to adopt a happy attitude. Begin by smiling at yourself in a mirror.

- Try to keep school problems at school. You can't take your students home—nor should you take their problems.

- Remind yourself that a bad day or a failed lesson doesn't mean that you a bad teacher. Remember that students will learn in spite of us.

- Diversify your activities so that in the non-school times, you have something to look forward to, perhaps taking part in a book club, gardening, or painting.

- Keep personal time limits. If you promise yourself an hour to read—take it.

- Plan for a personal monthly treat such as fresh flowers delivered to the school on a specific day each month. (I like to pay for all the deliveries at once. Then when they arrive, they seem like real treats.)

- Start a no-teach reach-out: a get-together with colleagues where teacher talk is strictly forbidden.

- Bring a healthy lunch and lots of water to school each day. Keep a water bottle on your desk.

- Buy a gym membership and use it. Consider this mandatory "me-time."

Some of the above ideas come from *Perfecting Your Private Practice* by Dr. Joan Neehall-Davidson.

18. Wisdom of Having a Mentor

… to assist you when you are feeling discouraged or down

Have you ever wished you had someone to talk to, to tell all your troubles to, and to provide you with an objective, empathetic response?

I have been a mentor several times and found it a positive experience. It wasn't until I needed an objective ear to listen to a particular concern of mine, however, that I realized I needed a mentor. I was fortunate enough to find one—not my husband, because, as a rule, a spouse cannot be objective—and since then my mentor and I have become good friends, able to serve as sounding boards for each other. Her advice is constructive and important to me.

Ten Ways to Find the Right Mentor

1. Begin by thinking about people that you admire and respect.
2. Choose someone with values similar to your own.
3. Before committing yourself to a relationship, enjoy a few casual get-togethers, to see how well you function together.
4. Establish a relationship of mutual respect. If you find this difficult, you may not yet have the right mentor.
5. Choose someone who is experienced and successful in life. Often, it is preferable for that person not to be in the educational profession so that you will gain an alternative outlook on situations.
6. Choose someone who is knowledgeable about your profession and its inherent difficulties and problems.
7. Check your comfort level with this person. If you cannot feel totally open, choose a different mentor.
8. Consider whether you can give some support back to your mentor. If you feel you cannot, seek a different mentor.
9. Approach the person openly. Explain your needs (someone to help you with decisions and listen) and judge from the person's reaction whether or not you have found the right mentor.
10. Once the arrangement is official (a decision usually made after two or three visits), ask yourself if you are learning (or giving) something every time you meet with your mentor. If not, work on a way to make this mutual exchange more effective by actively listening and asking pertinent questions.

Source: Adapted from *Perfecting Your Private Practice: Suggestions and Strategies for Psychologists,* by Dr. Joan Neehall-Davidson (Victoria, BC: Trafford Publishing, 2004)

19. Courage to Change

… at appropriate times during your career

Have you wanted to move to another school, but been stopped by fear of all the potential risks?

Mr. Park had taught at the same school for ten years. He was popular, established, and successful with the students. He was also restless and didn't know why. Then it occurred to him that he had gone as far as he could where he was—he had reached the pinnacle at his current school—and needed to change schools. At first, no one believed him. Why would he want to change when he had it so good where he was? In his heart, though, Mr. Park knew he needed to change. The first year at the new school wasn't easy, but in the long run the move was probably the best personal and career move Mr. Park ever made.

Ten Ideas of What to Do at a New School

1. When you move to a new school, bring only the necessities, such as favorite units, personal books, and teacher guides. Consider this a fresh start.
2. Take a year to establish yourself before volunteering for extracurricular activities or other tasks. Be patient with yourself and expect some initial nervousness and confusion.
3. Watch, listen, and learn. Every school has its own culture. You will need to fit it.
4. Get to know the support staff immediately. Learn their names and responsibilities. Remember that a supportive secretary can make your job a lot easier.
5. Do your homework before the move. Find out the dress code for teachers (every school is different), as well as the routines and school philosophy.
6. Be visible in the school—avoid hiding in your room.
7. Attend and observe as many of the school "extras"—sports games, concerts, presentations—as possible so that you will gain an idea of where your interests lie.
8. Try something new, perhaps a new subject, grade, reading series, or teaching strategy.
9. Keep a record of staff names, interests (as you discover them), pet peeves, and any other tidbits of information you come across. This familiarity will help you build the peer rapport necessary for successful teaching.
10. Write a letter to the families of the students you will be teaching. Introduce yourself and share some of your past experiences and your teaching philosophy.

Organization

Clutter, whether of classroom, desk, papers, vehicle, or mind, breeds stress. The ability to have everything in order and to systematize, be it as small as a desk or as large as an assembly of noisy students, is a definite strength needed for effective teaching.

Ideally, all teachers have and model for their students organizational skills. They can begin by organizing space and time and then facilitate learning by bringing curriculum and students together in ways that enable the students to function and grow well, yet leave teachers time for personal pursuits. Organization includes dealing with overactive minds, common enemies of sleep or relaxation, and with the control problems posed by large gatherings of students.

Organization of Space: Some teachers know where everything is—at least most of the time. They don't waste time seeking materials or rooting through boxes or files for missing documents. They have an everything-in-its-place attitude.

Organization of Time: Most teachers want more hours in the day to complete everything they would like to. The best teachers, however, end up with more accomplished and less time wasted. Feeling in control of every situation, they enjoy more tranquility, while their students experience authentic learning.

Organization of Mind: Teachers usually have so many plans and ideas rushing around in their heads that it can be difficult to "slow the brain" and focus on a single thought. Doing so, though, is an invaluable skill. If teachers can organize their busy brains, they will feel more peaceful and relaxed even when faced with many expectations at once.

Organization of Student Body: When students congregate, the chance of inappropriate behavior escalates exponentially with the number of bodies—not a time for teachers to behave in low-key or invisible fashion. Many adults feel uncertain about what to do, though. They resort to shouting or trying to be louder than unruly students, tactics that don't work. Teachers who establish and maintain order and supervision ensure positive group behavior and gain student respect.

20. Organization of Space

… of supplies, papers, assignments, and classroom information

Have you ever had the "where-did-I-put-that-important-form?" syndrome?

The teacher was sure she had put the list of marks in her Marks folder, but now it simply wasn't there. Panic mounted as she searched frantically through every drawer of her desk and every file folder in her cabinet. She needed those marks. She hadn't recorded them yet! Just when she was about to give up, the missing sheet of paper slipped off her plan book and fluttered to the floor. Saved! This time!

Ten Ways to Organize Space

1. Have specific places for everything. Use bins, colored folders, and labelled boxes for everything from books and papers to "show and tell" collections. Shoe caddies and pocket charts make excellent miscellaneous organizers.
2. Cut the clutter. Keep your desk free of piles of paper. Maximize workspace.
3. Avoid hoarding old lesson plans and materials. Discard any individual lessons or worksheets that have not been used in six months or units that have not been used in a year.
4. Keep a separate file folder for each student; put anything pertaining to the student in it immediately. Cull the files monthly.
5. Keep a personal bulletin board adjacent to your desk. Tack all contents from your mailbox or principal there as soon as you get them. Go through these weekly, culling or responding to them.
6. Assign students to organize and clean specific parts of the room on a regular basis.
7. Use a system of In/Out folders for assignments. Choose a separate color for each subject and keep the folders on a shelf or table (*not* on your desk). Consistently refuse to accept assignments in any other place.
8. Assign a particular place in the room where all materials for the day, such as worksheets and handouts, will be kept. At the end of each day, remove extras and put materials there for the next day.
9. Clean the interior of your car frequently. (Teachers tend to keep *everything* in the back seat or trunk.) Less clutter equals less stress.
10. Clean out your purse or briefcase regularly. Again, less clutter equals less stress.

21. Organization of Time
… including teaching and personal commitments

How often have you thought you'd never finish all of the required curriculum in any given year?

Mr. Parker was frazzled. It was the beginning of June. Already the students were in "summer mode" and he still had a huge chunk of curriculum to cover. He had to make a decision: skip most of the remaining curriculum, or try to force-feed it to the students in three weeks. Suddenly he thought about the past several years, and unhappily realized he faced the same conundrum every June. He wondered if all teachers were like him, but was too embarrassed to ask.

Ten Ways to Organize Time

1. Keep a personal timetable, organizer, or daily planner that you carry with you at all time. Log *everything*, including doctor appointments, upcoming school events, deadlines, and meetings.
2. Write *everything* on a large desk calendar—meetings, supervision responsibilities, upcoming school activities.
3. Establish routines for specific daily activities, such as taking attendance and preparing for recess. They will become organized habits.
4. Time everyday class activities, such as moving from one place in the school to another. Inform the students of how long they have to complete the move; then, ask them to try shortening it by a few seconds.
5. Practise making one activity serve two or more purposes. For example, dismiss students at recess by having each answer a quick question or repeat an important fact.
6. Always have instant activities ready for those difficult moments when work is finished, but there are still so many minutes until the bell. (See "Instant Activities," next page.)
7. Do your best to ensure that directions and instructions are succinct and clear. (See Providing Clear Directions, page 55.)
8. Consistently arrive at school early enough to prepare for the day. Teachers who arrive at the last minute are notoriously less effective.
9. Be a list maker. Prioritize the to-do items and check off daily what you have accomplished. (Scan your old lists when you feel you haven't accomplished anything!)
10. Avoid exceeding time guidelines you set for yourself. For example, if you allow yourself one hour for marking, but are not finished in that time, stop anyway and complete the marking in another self-allotted period.

Instant Activities

- Simple games such as Simon Says

- Word searches, puzzles, or mazes

- **Twenty Questions:** Keep a set of file cards with either trivia or learned fact questions in your desk.

- **Finger Facts:** In pairs or small groups, students shake closed fists three times, then open to reveal some fingers, the total number of fingers shown to equal a number called out by the teacher.

- **The Grand Old Duke of York** (a quick stand-up-sit-down):

  The Grand Old Duke of York,
  He had ten thousand men.
  He marched them UP to the top of the hill,
  and he marched them DOWN again.
  And when they were UP they were up.
  And when they were DOWN they were down.
  And when they were only HALFWAY UP,
  they were neither UP nor DOWN.

- **Partner Word Toss:** After the teacher provides a prompt, such as "fruits" or "items of clothing," students toss related words back and forth, until one falters.

- **Name Game:** The class takes turns saying each student's name with an accompanying adjective, for example, Pretty Patty. Or, students could say each name with an appropriate phrase: Good-at-math Patty.

- **Ice Cube Dance:** Everyone stands and for thirty seconds imagines that an ice cube has been dropped down his or her neck.

- **The Glad Game:** In small groups, students take turns responding to a sentence provided by the teacher and completing the phrase *I am glad …* For example, the teacher says, "Tomorrow is Friday," and students reply, "I am glad it's the last day of school," "I am glad we get gym tomorrow," "I am glad my family is going to the zoo on Saturday."

- **Thunderstorm:** Students rub their hands together for a few seconds, then click their fingers, clap lightly, clap more energetically, and finally rapidly hit their desks and stamp their feet. They reverse the actions to illustrate a storm leaving.

- **Alphabet Game:** Using the alphabet in sequence, students talk to a neighbor, with each piece of dialogue beginning with a word that starts with the next letter in sequence. Example: "*A* bug was on my lunch." "*B*ut you didn't eat it, did you?" "*C*ould you eat a bug?"

22. Organization of Mind

… to approach each task with a clear head

How often have you felt your head was about to burst with all the information, things to do, and student needs racing through your brain in a never-ending loop?

"You look terrible," Mr. Ludwick told the other teacher monitoring the hall with him.

"Thanks," was the mumbled reply. "Can't sleep."

"You sick?" Mr. Ludwick asked.

"Na—just too much stuff in my mind. You know how it is."

"Actually, I don't," Mr. Ludwick said. "I sleep like a baby."

"What's your secret?" the colleague yawned.

"I just tell myself as I get into bed that I'll think of all that stuff in the morning. It works for me."

"And then do you think of it in the morning?"

Mr. Ludwick smiled. "What difference does it make?" he said. "I get a good night's sleep."

Ten Ways to Organize Your Mind

1. Do your best to focus on one thing at a time, even if you are multi-tasking. Do this by purposefully forcing away thoughts of anything but the immediate task.
2. Use the "I'll-think-about-it-later" strategy. When you find many thoughts bombarding your brain, pick one, and tell yourself you'll think about the others in ten minutes (or half an hour or "later").
3. Sing. Join a choir or glee club or simply sing along with your car radio or a CD at home. Singing forces the mind to relax and release random thoughts.
4. Make notes diligently. When thoughts pop into your head, jot them down instead of allowing them to clutter your mind.
5. Experiment with pre-sleep techniques for uncluttering the active mind to find one that works for you. (See next page.)
6. If you wake during the night and a cluttered mind prevents you from returning to sleep, get up, have a warm drink (without caffeine), read something "light" for 15–20 minutes, then return to bed.
7. Practise "active listening," where you focus all your attention on the speaker to internalize and really *hear* what is being said.
8. During the day, practise simple at-your-desk exercises whenever you feel mind clutter bogging you down. (See next page.)
9. Go for a *brisk* walk, even just around the school, and focus on the environment.
10. Take a class in yoga, tai chi, or pilates and attend regularly.

Uncluttering the Mind

Getting Ready to Sleep
- Take a warm bath (not a shower) at the same time nightly.
- When you get into bed, take a series of three to ten deep breaths, holding each for as long as possible and releasing slowly.
- Avoid sugar or caffeine for two to three hours before bedtime.
- Try to go to bed at about the same time every night.
- Invest in a night-time eye mask. When worn, a mask provides a sense of peace and quiet.
- Some people relax with a glass of wine before bed. One glass serves the purpose.
- Try a warm milk drink, preferably not chocolate.
- If you understand yoga, practise a couple of the relaxation stretches before getting into bed. The "seated forward bend" (rag-doll slouch) or the "child's pose" work well.
- Read a book for pleasure just before retiring.

Relaxing the Body
All of these exercises can be done seated at your desk or even in your car. Often, when the mind is racing, the body is also tense. By reducing the physical tension even a little, the overactive head seems better able to relax. At the very least, the exercises will serve as an effective, temporary distraction.

- To reduce neck tension: On an exhalation, turn your head as far to one side as possible and look down over your shoulder. Hold for a few seconds. Inhale as you return to centre and repeat for other side.
- To reduce leg tension: Extend one leg away from body, foot flexed. On an exhalation, lean as far toward extended leg as possible and hold.
- To reduce anxiety: On an exhalation, slump forward onto your knees, rag-doll fashion, and hold.
- To release tension in back: Reach one arm down to the floor while the other stretches to the ceiling. Hold for twenty seconds.
- To reduce upper back fatigue: Squeeze shoulder blades as close together (behind you) as possible. Hold for five seconds. Pull shoulders as close to each other in the front as possible. Hold for five seconds. Repeat.
- To release back tension: Clasp hands in front, then push arms away from the body while inverting the hands (palms facing away from you). Hold.
- To reduce neck tension and headaches: Gently roll the head in a half circle from one side to the other with chin down to chest in mid-arc. Do not drop the head back.
- To reduce lower back stress: Contract abdominal muscles (pull belly button to backbone and then "down" to tailbone) and hold for as long as possible.
- To reduce anxiety: Close eyes and breathe in deeply (expand stomach, raise diaphragm). Hold for five seconds. Gently exhale through mouth, attempting to remove *all* residual air from lungs. (*Note:* If you cough, that's good!) Repeat several times. Use imagery to visualize yourself inflating and deflating like a balloon, and blowing out all stress on the exhalations.

23. Organization of Student Body

… at recess, noontime, assemblies, and class changes

Have you ever felt completely ineffective when faced with a huge mob of noisy students outside of your classroom?

As the 300 plus students forged toward the gym for the monthly assembly, Mrs. Paul shuddered. Today was her turn to monitor that crowd, and she never felt very effective when there were so many of them. Then the pushing started. At first just a tiny shove, then another, and soon the whole crowd was involved.

Just when she was about to start shouting, all the students froze and looked up. There, standing on a table, was little Mrs. Harrison—all five feet of her—with a "wand" in one hand.

"All right now," she said calmly and clearly, "that's better. I really wouldn't like to have turned you all into toads, you know. I expect all of you to walk in an orderly fashion …"

Mrs. Paul wondered why she hadn't been taught about the use of a make-believe wand when she was training to be a teacher.

Ten Ways to Help Control a Group of Students

1. Be visible. Keep moving through the student group.
2. Make eye contact with as many students as possible.
3. Use students' names where possible, in positive reinforcing ways. For example: "I like the way you are waiting quietly, Sharon."
4. Carry some sort of eye-catcher—an umbrella, a wand, a pretend sword, a cheerleader's pompom—or a noise-maker, such as a whistle or bell, to use if sound escalates.
5. Keep your voice calm when giving directions or mentioning inappropriate behavior. Avoid shouting.
6. *Expect* positive behavior from the students. You are more likely to get it.
7. Stand on something, such as a picnic table outside or a chair in the gym, to make you taller than the group.
8. Use nonverbal communication, such as slowly lowering both hands to indicate quiet.
9. Move quickly to any students who are causing a disturbance. That should prevent escalation of the inappropriate behaviors.
10. Ensure that there is an established school policy on how to deal with inappropriate group behavior and follow through with it immediately and consistently.

Appropriate Large-Group Student Behavior

- Line up with respect. That means no pushing or butting into line.

- Talk quietly or not at all, make sure that talk is appropriate, and listen for instructions.

- Watch the teacher in charge for directions.

- Wait patiently.

Consequences for Inappropriate Large-Group Behavior
Note: Generally, these are progressive consequences, the exception being for a severe misbehavior, such as hitting or fighting; in that case, the teacher should immediately invoke the third and fourth consequences listed.

- Warning by teacher in charge

- Removal of student from the group, to stand and remain beside the teacher

- Removal of student to the office with follow-up consequences, such as contacting parents or discussing issue with the principal or counsellor

- Restriction from taking part in large-group activities for a set time (To accompany this action, send a letter home. An outline appears below.)

Dear _____

This is to inform you that _____ has been restricted from attending assemblies and other large-group activities as a result of inappropriate behavior during (*activity*) _____ on (*date*) _____.

This expulsion will last until (*date when privileges resume*) _____.

During the event noted above, your child (*describe inappropriate behavior*) _____

_____

Below is your child's description of what happened. (*Student records the behavior with teacher/counsellor prompts.*) _____

Instead of attending the next activity of this nature, (*student's name*) _____ will (*describe alternate activity*) _____

Sincerely,

Teaching Strategies

Think of what you take away from a conference presentation or how you react to the initial impression the speaker had on you. Often, what we remember most are the beginning and ending of the presentation, and if the first impression made by the presenter was not good, we may not remember even those. There is an important lesson here: starting the day well and opening and closing lessons with pizzazz have a big impact on teaching success.

Beyond these featured teaching practices, I am discussing two relatively new strategies: teaching differentially and using picture books with older children. All of these strategies are visible attributes of powerful teaching.

Kick-Starting the Day: A school day often goes as well or as poorly as the first few moments; these precious minutes can be powerful enough to set the stage for whatever else is to come. The teacher who provides invigorating beginnings to the day will foster eager students and more fun in the class.

Opening a Lesson Well: It is best to capture the students' attention through a hook before beginning a lesson. Many teachers refer to such hooks as "motivational, or anticipatory, sets." I refer to them as "smart, powerful, teacher behavior." The teacher who uses hooks attracts student attention and enjoys personal satisfaction, pride, and confidence.

Closing a Lesson with Impact: Most of us remember how conversations, stories, movies, and activities begin and end better than we remember the medial details. The same is true for students. The teacher who makes good lesson closes capitalizes on this knowledge by providing students with an immediate summary of learning or behavior, strengthening accountability for learning.

Teaching to Diversities: Students do not learn in the same way; nor do they come to class with the same preparation, ability, culture, and motivation. As a result, teachers must tap into the power of differential teaching to reach and teach to the diversity in their classrooms, which seems to increase all the time. Teaching differentially leads to more student success and parental support, as well as less student frustration and personal disappointment.

Using Picture Books with Older Students: All teachers have experienced reluctant and struggling readers—the students who either won't or can't read. Some people frown upon the idea of providing these students with books below their "supposed" reading level; however, if the books are presented with passion and enthusiasm, and the follow-up activities are authentic and stimulating, their use will lead to further reading for many students.

24. Kick-Starting the Day

… with more than a smile and a "hello"

Have you ever noticed how first thing in the morning some students come in with a smile, but others drag themselves to their desks looking like they would rather be anywhere but there?

The students were huddled outside the school eagerly waiting for the bell to allow them entrance. The teacher on supervision wandered over to them to see why they appeared so excited to get to class and overheard students talking.

"I wonder what it'll be today?" the first said.

"I bet it'll be a joke," replied another.

"Nope!" put in a third. "It was a joke on Tuesday. Gotta be different today!"

When the teacher inquired about what the students were discussing, one of them told her, "It's the morning kick-start! It's cool!"

Ten Ways to Kick-Start the Day

1. Occasionally greet students at the door with a handshake and address each one by name. (*Good morning, Miss Jones.*)

2. Have a minimal cues message waiting on the board for them to solve immediately. For example: To_ _ y we _re going to _ _ _ gy_ to p_ _ _ b _ll.

3. Feature a cartoon or joke on the overhead for students to see when they enter.

4. Meet students at the door wearing a hat that will fit with a particular lesson during the day. Keep them in suspense until the lesson.

5. Begin the day by reading a humorous poem, such as one from *Where the Sidewalk Ends,* by Shel Silverstein.

6. Display a chant or short song on the board or overhead. Teach it immediately and begin the day with the group chanting it.

7. Have the pole and noose for the game Hangman drawn large on the board. Before they do anything else, students must figure out one thing they will be doing that day by playing this game.

8. Begin with a brief naming activity where each student says his or her name and a greeting of choice. Examples: "Hi, I'm Anna." "Cheers from Derek." "Yo, bro, Cal here."

9. On a rotating basis, let students take attendance "the old-fashioned way" by calling out names and checking. Add your name to the list, so that you must answer "present" too. The attendance-taker gains a sense of worth.

10. Model an unusual greeting—a salute, bow, curtsey, "alien" expression, "Yo," "Top of the morning," or "Greetings"—when meeting students at the door, and encourage them to respond the same way.

25. Opening a Lesson Well

… so that all of the students are engaged to learn

Have you ever thought that you spend more time "getting ready to teach" than teaching?

The students were silent. They sat in awe, wide eyes focused on the teacher who was quietly and slowly digging around in a big, brown-paper shopping bag. What would she bring out? They knew that as soon as that bag showed up, something interesting was going to appear from it. Suddenly, out popped a miniature statue of the Sphinx. There was a mutual gasp. "Yeah!" one student shouted with joy, "Today we get to write about Egypt."

Ten Ways to Open a Lesson Well

1. Begin by capturing the attention of all with a well-established cue, such as a particular sound, maybe a whistle, bell, or piece of music, or a visual signal, perhaps a hand raised.
2. Use "wait time." Avoid starting until all students are attending.
3. Use the brown-bag technique by drawing from the bag surprise items pertaining to the lesson.
4. Use a colored overhead in a darkened room. Ask students to observe it silently for thirty seconds and to speculate about why it's there.
5. Wear a hat that is specific to the lesson or subject. (One teacher always wore an Italian beret when it was time for students to do art.)
6. Provide a few general clues that invite students to guess what they will be doing. "It's Science. We'll look at something that has an effect on how we come to school." (weather)
7. Tie the lesson to students' interests. For example: If teaching a lesson on long division, begin by inviting students to think of anything—candies, hamburgers, baseball cards, bracelets, movie passes—they would like to have 100 of. Ask them to use their "choices" in such tasks as dividing the 100 items among twelve friends. Or, if the task is a writing project, provide an umbrella theme, perhaps adventure, then allow students to choose specific topics, such as camping or playing hockey.
8. Explain the purpose of the lesson. Students are more interested if they know why they are doing something.
9. Explain your expectations for the lesson. At the lesson outset, tell students exactly what they will be expected to do.
10. Use alert, confident body language and demonstrate passion for what you are about to teach or share.

26. Closing a Lesson with Impact

... instead of just "working till the bell"

The teacher was watching her Grade 6 students leave at the end of the day when she heard James ask Billy, "Did we have Social Studies homework?"

Billy replied, "Did we even have Social Studies today?"

The teacher sighed. So much for what she thought was a powerful lesson about governments leaving an impact.

How often have you been in the middle of a sentence when the bell sounds and students start packing up and rushing off?

Ten Ways to Close a Lesson with Impact

1. Watch the time and leave two or three minutes for closure.
2. Insist that students spend a few seconds in silent reflection to encourage information retention.
3. Ask students to jot down what they learned in their journals.
4. Provide an oral summary of the lesson. (See STOP below.)
5. Invite students to do the summary orally. (*Tell me what we talked about ... Summarize for me ...*)
6. Call for a silent response from every student. (*Close your eyes and summarize in your head.*)
7. Link the closing to your opening activity. (*We started today by ... and we learned that ...*)
8. Note the relevance of the lesson. (*We just learned that ... because ... This ... will help us when ...*)
9. Invite students to pair up and share what they just learned.
10. If time has truly run out, then at the least quickly say what you have just done.

S	"We **S**tarted the lesson ..."
T	"The **T**opic (Theme) was ..."
O	"Our **O**pportunities for practice were ..."
P	"The **P**urpose of learning this is ..."

27. Teaching to Diversities

… so that all your students have equal opportunity to learn

"What a motley crew! How can I ever reach them all when they are all so different?" How often have you looked at your class and thought that?

After her first day in Mrs. Klein's class, the student teacher said in amazement, "I didn't realize you taught a special needs class. And I thought there were fewer kids in special classes."

Mrs. Klein smiled. "It's not a special class," she said. "This is a normal Grade 4 class. All classes these days have very diverse populations. But they are all great kids, and their differences make our classroom all the richer."

Ten Ways to Teach a Diverse Population in the Class

1. Allow students to complete tasks at their own rates. That may mean providing extra time for some, additional activities for others.
2. Allow students choices about how they complete a task, whether they work alone or with a peer, and where they do the work.
3. Implement peer modelling, where capable students work with less capable ones and model the correct way to carry out a task or activity. (Remember to change partners often.)
4. Use Step Demos. Explain that you will fully demonstrate the task, such as making a mind map, and that students may choose to begin on their own at whatever step in your demonstration they feel capable. Those who are experiencing difficulty will wait until the demonstration is over, but some will begin almost immediately. Once you have finished making and describing what you are doing, leave your model as a sample.
5. Use Step Scaffolding. Similar to Step Demos, this process allows students to "fly solo" whenever they are ready or to stay with the teacher for continued assistance. The difference between this and a step demo is that with scaffolding, the teacher may not complete the entire process, but pull away as soon as students are on their own and provide intermittent help to individuals, as needed. For example, to teach students to print the letter "B," the teacher would say, *Put your pencil on the top line* (demonstrates), *then make a straight line to the bottom line* (demonstrates). *Put your pencil back at the top and make a clockwise circle to the midline* (does not demonstrate). *What do you think we do next?*
6. Encourage cooperative learning, which recognizes that students learn from each other.
7. Change expectations for students. For example, slower students may do only every other question or every third one, or write one paragraph rather than an entire essay.
8. Use prompting techniques that are specifically geared to struggling students. For example, word your questions for *yes* or *no* responses as opposed to open-ended ones for the rest of the class.
9. Discuss and demonstrate a variety of ways to respond to a question or complete a task in order to accommodate diverse student backgrounds.
10. Once directions have been given (see Providing Clear Directions, page 55), simplify them one more time for strugglers, ESL students, or others with individual needs.

28. Using Picture Books with Older Students

... not only to turn them on to reading, but also to captivate and stimulate them

How often have you struggled to find a book an older student (aged ten or up) will read independently, enjoy completely, and actually want to respond to?

"I don't read," Tyler announced on the second day of the school year.

"Of course you do," Mr. Gates said.

"Nope! I don't!"

Mr. Gates looked at the lanky 12-year-old and sighed. *Another reluctant reader. Now what?*

That night when Mr. Gates was reading a particularly funny children's picture book to his young son, he got an idea. The next day he enthusiastically introduced the picture book to his Grade 7 class and invited them to become involved in a variety of interesting projects based on the book. He was thrilled when Tyler picked up the book and began to skim through it. Step one—accomplished!

Ten Ways of Using Picture Books with Older Students

1. Share your personal interest in picture books. Give the students a few significant reasons such as "they are so colorful" or "they always have a good lesson."

2. Introduce the book with excitement and pizzazz. For example, assume an excited pose, hands up and fingers spread, and call out briskly and fairly loudly "da da da da!" or hide the book from view and announce, "This is going to be soooooo great!" Students' reactions will depend entirely on your ability to present the book well.

3. Be sure to display and talk about the best illustrations or pictures in the book so that students can enjoy them and see how they contribute to understanding the text.

4. Practise reading the story ahead of time so that you can maintain eye contact during reading. Doing so will increase enthusiasm for the book.

5. Prepare students for the reading by explaining that although the book was designed for younger students, you have an idea of how they can use it for some exciting projects.

6. Before reading, provide a purpose for the session by telling students what to listen for. For example, almost all picture books have a lesson or moral—invite the students to figure it out. Or, ask them to listen for any clues about the main character's personality.

7. To avoid breaking engagement with the story, read it through without interruption. Follow with a second reading during which you stop periodically to point out interesting illustrations. Draw attention to detail. For example, discuss the art of book illustration and consider how difficult or easy it might have been in this book.

8. Stop every once in a while to ask questions such as "How do you think young children would feel at this part?" You thereby reassure your students that you still consider them "older" even though you are sharing children's literature.

9. When you have finished reading, leave the book in the silent reading area of your room.

10. Suggest a variety of possible reader responses that will directly involve students in authentic reactions to the book, and also provide an audience, a younger class, for these responses. (See "Reader Responses to Picture Books," next page.)

Reader Responses to Picture Books

- Discuss *dependent authorship*, where students write in the style of the author, and invite students to devise alternative endings or "sequels" to the book.

- Invite students to write Dear Abby questions and answers based on book content. The questions and answers should be relevant to younger children and shared with them.

- Have students rewrite the story, using the same theme of the book, in language more appropriate for students their age, or even for adults or seniors. For example, students could write personal narratives related to their own families in response to *Where the Wild Things Are*, which has a theme of being aware of what's important, in this case, family. Let them share their stories with the chosen age group.

- Invite students to rewrite the book without benefit of the pictures; what happens in the pictures will have to be explained in words.

- Tell students they are going to "sell" the book. They must create posters, blurbs, and advertising materials, to promote the book to younger children. Post these materials in their classes; then, do follow-up to see how many students read the book as a result.

- Invite students to rewrite the book as a ballad. For example, the text from each page (or more, depending on the book) could be transcribed into rhyming couplets. The basic story would remain the same, but the presentation would be a long, narrative poem.

- Have students prepare a drama presentation of the book, perhaps with puppets, shadow plays, mime, or tableaux, to present to students in younger grades.

- As an alternate task, particularly relevant to students less enthralled by writing, suggest making a video or radio play of the book. Share with students in younger grades.

- Have students research young adult books that have themes similar to the ones presented in a particular picture book. For example, using *Where the Wild Things Are* again, students would read books related to the importance of family.

- Work with a teacher of younger students to create buddy pairs, where your students read the book with the younger students.

Communication

Communication is far more than just talking. It encompasses the signals teachers send by looks and appearance, the directions they give, the way they read aloud, and the manner in which they pace lessons, report to parents, and talk to volunteers and classroom aides.

Monitoring Nonverbal Communication: Nonverbal communication, often easily understood, is everything teachers do and show to others. Students are experts at deciphering teachers' nonverbal cues; therefore, teachers need to master nonverbal communication to gain more student attention and communicate well.

Providing Clear Directions: Consider how many times a day you tell students what to do, where to go, which book to select, and so on. Then think how many minutes are lost in retelling. Even with the best directions, it happens sometimes. Good directions lead to more on-task behavior from students, less time wasted, and less frustration.

Managing Timing and Pacing: Taking a brisk approach to instruction, making well-thought-through presentations, using wait-times, and providing clear directions all help to fully involve the students. They also permit the teacher to model the importance of authentic time management and to show students respect by being prepared for them. The results of good timing and pacing include more productive activity and more focused students.

Reading Aloud Fluently: Reading aloud to students does more than allow them to enjoy literature. It is a good teaching strategy that models fluent reading and voice control. It enables listeners to benefit from writing above their independent reading level and it helps to develop the class as community.

Dealing Effectively with Aides and Volunteers: With their eyes, ears, hands, and minds, aides and volunteers can add punch to the teacher's teaching power; however, direct communication with them is necessary. One common complaint they make is that they did not know what the teacher expected. Clear direction can lead to more cohesion in the classroom and more student work completed.

Talking Openly to Parents or Guardians: Not all parents are equally receptive, and not all students have only "positives" about which to talk. The teacher who handles these situations well enjoys more parental support and student accountability and less undone homework.

29. Monitoring Nonverbal Communication
… in the classroom, halls, school grounds, and staff room

Have you ever watched a colleague and been amazed at how her body language didn't match her facial expression?

"I don't think Ms. Smith is mad," Janice remarked to Heather as they left the class. "I think she was just, you know, warning us."

"Absolutely she was mad," Heather replied. "Furious!"

"How can you say that?" countered Janet. "She was smiling when we left."

"Didn't you see her eyes?" Heather said. "They were mean looking. She was mad all right!"

Ten Ways to Improve Nonverbal Communication

1. Practise open body language (relaxed posture, arms at sides, hands open) for everyday interactions.
2. For everyday teaching, use animated talk by incorporating gestures such as head nods, hand movements, and changes in body orientation. If you fail to do this, students may see you, or the lesson, as boring.
3. When you are giving directions, use forceful body language (eye contact made, body and stance alert, head high) to indicate the information's level of importance.
4. When dealing with inappropriate behavior, demonstrate level of concern by incorporating more rigid, formal body language. Move a bit closer (but remember that culture dictates a comfortable distance), and hold eyes, mouth, and stance firm.
5. When seated and talking one-to-one with a student or colleague, lean slightly forward, maintain eye contact, bend your head slightly to the side, and keep your hands open and on your uncrossed knees.
6. To gain the attention of a group, scan quickly, looking at each member, if possible, and proceed once you have gained eye contact.
7. Change your voice tone, pitch, volume, and speed to match your nonverbal communication. For example, speak slowly and softly when offering words of private encouragement, fast and high pitched when sharing something exciting.
8. Listen to what is not being said by watching the speaker closely. For example, why is a student telling you he is going to skip school tomorrow? Watch for signals of discomfort, such as leg swinging, finger kneading or clicking, and gaze aversion.
9. Practise little, everyday actions, such as shaking hands. For example, to shake hands, stand about one metre apart, posture straight, arm bent at the elbow; make eye contact, and use a firm grip.
10. Practise erect posture and straight head position when instructing or providing information. (Check your posture when you are tired or upset.) Erect posture and a raised head held high show authority and confidence, and instill confidence in others.

30. Providing Clear Directions

… so that students know all the details of your expectations

"What are we supposed to do, teacher?" How often do you hear that classroom question asked every day?

I had just finished giving what I considered very clear directions for the interesting writing task when questions began.

> *"Do we do this in our language journals?"*
>
> *"Can I do it at home on my computer?"*
>
> *"Hey, can I use a word processor too?"*
>
> *"How many words is it supposed to be?"*
>
> *"Is this for marks?"*
>
> *"How do we start? I'm stuck! I can't get started!"*
>
> *"Teacher, what are we supposed to do? I forget."*

I sighed and realized that my directions were not as clear as I had thought. I vowed to do better in the future.

Ten Steps to Providing Clear Directions

1. Be sure *you* know exactly what your directions are. (Practise saying them to yourself or write them in your plans.)
2. Word the directions simply and concisely.
3. Use "baby steps." Break down the task.
4. Provide directions in more than one modality. Write them on a chart, overhead, or board *and* give them orally. Just writing a page number down offers visual clarity.
5. Add to the directions a statement telling the students *exactly* what to do when finished with the assigned task. Suggest how long the task should take.
6. Explain what consequence will follow if the task is not finished in the allocated time.
7. Have students turn to a neighbor and repeat the directions.
   - What will you do first?
   - Next?
   - When you are finished?
   - If you don't finish?
8. Move to slow learners or any students with specific diversities once others have begun to work and clarify directions.
9. If necessary, arrange for "starter buddies." These are partners whose sole job is to see that each other is "on track."
10. Teach students that, once you have given directions and clarified them to the point where you are sure they all understand, they may not ask for them again. You are giving them the responsibility of listening.

Sample Oral Directions:

We are going to be writing a report in our science journals. You will need to get out your pencils, your science journals, and your notes from yesterday's experiment. You will have 20 minutes to write. When finished, put your journals in the Hand-in box, and silently read the last of Chapter 3 in your science text. Now, what will you do first?

Directions on Board:

1. (What?) Science journals, pencils, lab notes
2. (How long?) 20 min.
3. (Finished?) Hand in, then complete Ch. 3

31. Managing Timing and Pacing
… in delivery of lessons, assignments, and directions

How many times have you found yourself rushing like mad to finish a lesson before the bell, or, on the other hand, struggling to fill time when you have nothing planned?

Note from a Parent:

Dear Mr. Knowles,

Thanks for getting me to work on time every day. You see, I always had trouble getting up and ready for work, until Josh got in your class. He says you are a "real nut" for being on time and he sure doesn't want to be late for your class because he's afraid he'll miss something. So, that's why I'm not late for work anymore—Josh makes me get up.

Ten Ways to Achieve Effective Timing and Pacing

1. Always plan well. "Winging it" usually leads to chaotic pacing and either running out of time for completion or having too much time left to "fill."
2. Be in the class before the bell rings.
3. Talk at a brisk pace. Slow, monotonous speech puts students to sleep.
4. Use wait-for-attention time effectively. Before beginning, use a cue or signal to show you are waiting, then pause a few seconds until all eyes are on you.
5. Write directions on a board before students enter or while they are busy. Alternatively, you could use an overhead. Avoid having your back to students, especially while talking.
6. Move around the room when talking. Try to stand close to every child once during the day. Your movement around the room tends to keep the pace of the class up.
7. Model punctual behavior. Always begin and end class on time, following a good lesson close. (See Closing a Lesson with Impact, page 49.)
8. Insist on receiving assignments on time and return them in a timely fashion. You thereby set an example for efficient use of time. Discuss the consequences of handing in late and enforce them consistently. (See "Consequences for Late Assignments" next page.)
9. Allow short "refocusing" breaks during long or difficult lessons. Doing so serves to speed up the lesson and the learning curve.
10. Purposely include think time and wait time when providing new or difficult material, or after asking a question. Allow students a few silent moments (about thirty seconds) to reflect on concepts or ideas.

Consequences for Late Assignments

It is important to keep the consequences as authentic to the late assignment as possible.

- The student loses a percentage of the mark.

- The student is expected to remain after school or at lunch to complete the assignment as well as a related task. For example, for a late essay, ask the student to write a "hook" and "thesis statement" for another topic.

- The student is expected to complete in-school work as closely related to the late assignment as possible. For example, for late math work, the student assists the teacher after school the next time the teacher has to do an accounting-type task.

- Parents or guardians are notified *by* the student of the problem.

- The student is required to keep a diary for a week, showing how his or her time is spent, then to create a "Homework Plan" to be kept on record. This plan will specifically document how much time will be spent daily on homework, where it will be done, and so on.

- The student is expected to report to the school counsellor to discuss reasons for the late assignment.

- The student is expected to write a report about tardiness and its effect, for example, a surgeon being late for surgery or a school custodian being late to open the school.

- The student is expected to write an explanation of any difficulties or problems that led to the assignment being turned in late, then suggest possible ways to overcome these in the future.

- The student whose assignment was late is required to come up with an appropriate consequence for the inconvenience to the teacher. For example, the student may offer to help the teacher with a particular after-school task, such as tidying up the classroom, to free some time for the teacher to mark the late assignment.

32. Reading Aloud Fluently
… to students of all ages, every day

Have you ever wondered if students were really listening when you read aloud to them? Have you ever asked yourself if you were "interesting" to listen to?

Note from a former student (19 at time of writing):

Dear Mrs. Morton,

I just wanted to let you know that I am working at the hospital in ___, just like you suggested, and I love it. But mostly I wanted to tell you that I still remember lots of what we did in class, especially the books and stories you read to us. Those were the best. You know I wasn't a good reader back then (I'm better now) and every day I could hardly wait for you to read. That made my day. Thanks.

    Your ex-student in Grade 7,
    Kevin Stiles

Ten Ways to Approach Reading Aloud Fluently

1. Using an enthusiastic voice to increase motivation for listening, share the purpose of the reading session. If it is purely for enjoyment, say so, then avoid asking questions or expecting responses.
2. Provide students with "ownership" of the reading by allowing them to choose a book or story from several you have selected.
3. Practise reading aloud to a spouse, friend, or colleague. Ask for constructive criticism and then act on it. Alternatively, read and record your voice on audiotape. Listen critically for ways to improve your oral presentation.
4. Finger-point the text while reading aloud, so you can look up, make eye contact, and keep your place. (You also model a technique for reading fluency.)
5. Use expressive and varied enunciation, pitch and voice levels at appropriate places—avoid monotone robotic reading. For example, whisper, then raise your voice to high volume and pitch as excitement rises.
6. Maintain interest through pacing and timing. Read some parts slowly, others quickly. Stop reading *before* the assigned time is up if interest is flagging; read a bit longer if interest is high.
7. Accentuate parts of the reading through nonverbal communication, such as hand gestures, facial expressions, and posture positions.
8. Incorporate guided imagery into the session. Pause and ask students to put themselves into the story as you read, or at the end of the reading session, guide them through a series of steps based on the story setting.
9. Stop at appropriate parts and share personal feelings. (*That part made me feel very sad for the main character.*)
10. Provide reading/listening time despite any earlier inappropriate behavior.

33. Dealing Effectively with Aides and Volunteers

… on a regular or intermittent basis

If you have worked with an aide, have you ever despaired of actions taken as a result of miscommunication? If you haven't worked with an aide, have you ever wondered if you should?

Taken from a list of "pet peeves" of aides and volunteers:

- *Lack of honest communication between the teacher and aide*
- *Don't understand what the teacher wants me to do*
- *The teacher doesn't support me when I make a decision.*
- *The teacher doesn't tell me when I've done something well, but she sure tells me when I haven't.*
- *She [teacher] keeps changing her mind and doesn't keep me informed.*

Ten Ideas for Dealing Effectively with Aides and Volunteers

1. If possible, before they arrive, acquaint yourself with the qualifications, experience, and likes/dislikes of the helpers. Ask, if you need to.
2. Allow a few minutes to explain your expectations of the helper, and provide a "quick copy"—a written list or description of what you want done. Use clear directions, just as you do with students. (See Providing Clear Directions, page 55.)
3. Show politeness, respect, and appreciation—helpers are not servants.
4. Tell helpers what "fun" thing you want them to do at the same time you ask for help in more mundane areas. They will be more likely to come back.
5. Be alert to personality mixes and group kids accordingly. Ensure that helpers work with more than tough or slow kids. Communicate reasons for your chosen mixes.
6. Avoid leaving helpers alone in class at any time.
7. Support your helpers if a negative situation arises. Explain your stance on behavior, and tell exactly what you do and when you do it.
8. Be prepared to model appropriate ways to talk to and with students for the helpers as well as for the students. Helpers will take their cues from what you do and how you react.
9. Give your helpers the same breaks as you get. Discuss breaks with them, allowing them to choose times, if possible.
10. At the end of the time with a helper, acknowledge your appreciation by specifically stating what the helper did that was of benefit to you and your class. (*I liked the way you were able to help___. He never would have been able to complete this project without you.*)

34. Talking Openly to Parents or Guardians
… throughout the year as well as at official reporting times

Do you dread parent-teacher interviews? Do you struggle to come up with the best way to inform parents or guardians of a child's difficulties, or to find something positive to say, and mean it?

A new teacher, during her first parent-teacher interviews, faced the ultimate challenge. A parent—himself the principal of another school—confronted her unfairly and created a highly stressful situation. The teacher felt cornered and found she was attempting to justify actions unnecessarily. She ended up apologizing for just about everything and left the interview with every intention of quitting teaching right then and there. Luckily, an empathetic colleague prevented this from happening.

Ten Suggestions for Talking Openly and Effectively to Parents or Guardians

1. For scheduled meetings, know what you want to say and how you want to say it. Be well prepared.
2. For the meeting find a quiet spot where no one will disturb or interrupt you.
3. Speak in a clear, concise manner, maintaining eye contact and listening actively to what the parent says. Be alert to body language—both yours and the parent's—and based on these, take cues for concluding or extending the talk.
4. Always begin by attempting to make the parent feel at ease. Smile, make eye contact, offer to shake hands, and call the parent by name (Mr. _____ or Mrs. _____).
5. Before identifying areas of concern, ask the parent to share concerns or questions. If these are similar to yours, build on what has been said by first paraphrasing the parent, then agreeing.
6. If the parent's concerns differ from yours, acknowledge and deal with them before introducing any of your own. Validate the parent's feelings by accepting them. (*I understand your concern …*)
7. Before verbalizing a concern, outline a student strength or improvement. Show work examples to support this or cite specific behavior examples.
8. Note no more than two major concerns at any one session. If there are many concerns, then prioritize. Overwhelming the parent will not help the student. Provide specific examples to support your claims.
9. Provide the parent with alternatives or actions to help the student improve. Remember that you are the professional, and the parent looks to you for suggestions and guidance.
10. Conclude the talk positively by summarizing what has been discussed; reviewing the plan of action, if there is one; and thanking the parent for coming.

Classroom Management

There is no doubt that more learning occurs in a well-managed classroom than in an unruly one. Every teacher wants to have good classroom management (as opposed to "control," which implies a dictatorship-like atmosphere) so that students feel a sense of ownership and personal pride in the room. The challenge of achieving good classroom management never ends.

By taking proactive measures, a good teacher can avoid some classroom management problems that may accompany, for instance, changing from in-class mathematics to in-gym physical education. Suggestions for making low-key responses, and also for defusing the proverbial power struggle, should it arise, have been included.

Using Low-Key Management Techniques: Teachers who move smoothly from teaching to low-key intervention back to teaching enjoy classes of students who are more on task and avoid use of higher level management techniques.

Making Smooth Transitions: Teachers know how much time is lost daily in the transition from subject to subject, room to room, book to book, and so on—and how the risk of inappropriate behavior rises at these times; however, planning for smooth transitions often gets lost in the shuffle of daily responsibilities. Making smooth transitions results in more time on task, quiet classrooms, and a sense of class momentum.

Aiding Struggling Stragglers: There are some in every class: the students who always seem to be behind. If a teacher chooses to ignore them, or, worse still, berate them for their tardiness, the potential for disruptive behavior is great. The teacher who helps struggling stragglers enjoys more student successes, more classroom cohesiveness, and greater personal satisfaction.

Defusing a Power Struggle: While no hard-and-fast rules for dealing with explosive situations, commonly called "power struggles," apply—every child is unique; therefore, every situation—I share a few classroom-tested ideas. The teacher who handles a power struggle well experiences more inner tranquility and ensures that students take responsibility for their actions.

Forming Random Groups: Teachers know the difficulties that forming flexible, non-homogeneous groups can cause. They are familiar with "Can I be in ___'s group?" and "I don't want to be with ___." There is a way around this. Early in the year explain that all groups will be formed by you and that everyone will, at some time, work with everyone else. Then use a variety of ideas to make this happen in quick, creative, teacher-controlled ways.

35. Using Low-Key Management Techniques
... that help to keep the class focused and on task

How often have you resorted to screaming at your class to get them on task, and then felt a tad incapable as a result?

"I like Ms. Marble. She never yells," announced a smiling seven-year-old.

"Lucky you. Mrs. Shaw yells all the time," a peer complained.

"Does that work? Does it make you all be quiet?"

"Mostly it just makes us yell louder."

"Hmmm. I think Ms. Marble is better than Mrs. Shaw at making kids behave and do good stuff."

"Me too. Wish I had Ms. Marble."

Ten Ways to Use Low-Key Management Techniques

1. Use the "one-minute-talk" technique. When students are restless and chattering, tell them they have one minute from your start cue to your end cue, during which time they *must* talk. Works like a charm.
2. Use proximity. Move to an off-task student but avoid calling his name or embarrassing him.
3. Develop a rapport with "difficult" or reluctant students. Get to know them personally as well as from a "learning" point of view.
4. Circulate when students are working. Avoid the temptation to sit at your desk and mark.
5. Use nonverbal cues, such as a frown or crossed arms, when one or two students are off task.
6. Anticipate misbehavior and deal with it inconspicuously. Avoid making it the centre of attention.
7. Use I-messages when explaining your expectations: *I need ... I want ... I expect ...*
8. Make positive descriptions of expected behaviors. (*We will carry out this task with only quiet talk,* as opposed to *There will be no loud talking.*)
9. Explain how misbehaviors personally affect you or make you feel. (*When you do that, I have to stop my instructions. I feel upset when you ... because I have to ...*)
10. Adopt the "stepping-on-my-last-nerve" technique. Find an obvious form of nonverbal communication that lets students know that they have pushed you as far as you can go.

36. Making Smooth Transitions

… when changing subjects, physical locations, or the direction the class is moving

Have you ever thought your class was going beautifully until you asked them to put away one set of books and take out another?

Ms. Robertson tapped her chime. In an instant, the students stopped what they were doing, all eyes on the teacher. "Thank you," she said quietly. "It's circle time. Your record is 30 seconds. Do you think you can beat that today?" Eager heads nodded and murmured "yesses" filled the room, but no one moved.

Ms. Robertson tapped the chime again. Suddenly, the whole class seemed to move as one, each student silently pushing a desk to the edge of the room, leaving the centre empty. Then the class quickly and quietly sat in a circle in the emptied area.

"Great!" Ms. Robertson cried, clapping her hands. "Twenty-eight seconds. A new record!"

Ten Ways to Make Smooth Transitions

1. Keep all transitions as brief as possible and plan ahead for them. (Know exactly what you want students to do.)
2. Always have all materials ready before class.
3. Establish and reinforce rules for entering, leaving, and beginning a class. Train students to respond to a "moving signal" and rehearse the actions.
4. Establish and reinforce procedures for routine tasks, such as the taking of attendance.
5. Plan more material than you think you need so that there is no unexpected down time.
6. Arrange the classroom for efficient movement of desks, students, and equipment.
7. Create and post a daily schedule and review this with your students.
8. Complete and clarify instructions before relinquishing student attention. (*Don't move until …*)
9. Provide and stick to a time limit for the transition. Adopt the "beat your own time" concept. Kids love it and become experts quickly.
10. Always plan for down time. (*When you are finished, you will …*)

SCORE: Perfect Transitions

S	Simplicity (of directions)
C	Consistency (of directions)
O	Organization (of actions)
R	Reinforcement (of behaviors)
E	Exactness (of directions)

37. Aiding Struggling Stragglers

… in a quiet, non-threatening manner to help them "catch up"

How often have you told yourself that if it wasn't for ___ and ___ in your class, you'd have a perfect group?

"You haven't even started your essay," Mrs. Hughes said quietly to John. "What's up?"

"I'm not gonna do it," John replied firmly.

*"Unacceptable," Mrs. Hughes said matter-of-factly. "Let's talk about this. How much **will** you do?"*

"The first sentence."

Mrs. Hughes appeared to consider this, then said, "Nope. Not good enough. I need more. How about the first two paragraphs?"

"No way," John muttered. Then, getting into the "game," he offered, "How about one paragraph?"

*"One **good** paragraph?" Mrs. Hughes asked. John nodded. They shook hands and John began writing his paragraph.*

Ten Ways to Help a Straggler

1. Solve the mystery. Try to find out why the student is behind—lack of confidence, missed skills or strategies, physical fatigue—and deal with your findings appropriately.

2. Reassess the needs of the particular student. Does he really need to do twenty questions, or can he get by with ten? Consider the minimum you will expect or he will need for success, and ask for only that.

3. Reinforce "partial completions." Discuss what has been done, as opposed to what has not.

4. Make a prioritized list of all the areas or tasks in which the student is behind. Discuss this with her and strongly consider "wiping the slate clean" and offering a fresh start. (Sometimes, being far behind is so daunting that catch-up is impossible.) Alternatively, pick one or two important tasks to complete.

5. Offer individual or small-group tutorials at a regular time and place every week.

6. Use a barter contract (as in the anecdote above). Point out what is expected, ask the student how much he is willing or able to do, and come to an agreement about what will be completed. Increase your expectations a little at a time.

7. Seat the straggler close to a faster student, and encourage them to help each other. (One benefits in a practical way; the other, in the positive feeling that comes from helping a peer and from being appreciated by you.)

8. Consider giving the straggler an older student buddy, someone who comes to your class for a few minutes daily to help the straggler get organized and get going.

9. As soon as directions have been given, move to the straggler. Quietly and respectfully, provide more start-up motivation: for example, clarify directions, check for understanding, and check for necessary materials.

10. Keep parents informed of your efforts to help the straggler, but avoid burdening them with numerous areas in which the straggler is behind. This is your problem, not theirs.

38. Defusing a Power Struggle

… or any potentially explosive situation in the classroom

When did you last experience panic when a classroom situation suddenly escalated into that feared power struggle? Were your first thoughts, "Oh, oh, what do I do now?"

It had become a shouting match—teacher and student! Kendra's misbehavior had finally pushed Mrs. White too far and the battle of wills was on. The louder Mrs. White reprimanded, the louder Kendra shouted back. Soon Kendra had toppled her desk and stormed from the room, Mrs. White right behind her.

By the time the principal and several colleagues had appeared, Kendra had broken a window and cut both herself and the teacher. Mrs. White felt terrible. She knew she should have done something differently; she just didn't know what!

Ten Ways to Defuse a Power Struggle

1. If the student is still showing some semblance of control, offer pencils and paper and invite him to write or illustrate how he feels. If he wants to, he can tear the paper up.
2. Invite the student to take a speed walk either to a specific location, such as a washroom, and back, or once around the school.
3. Invite the student to imagine blowing a balloon up with his anger—then popping it.
4. Suggest use of a pre-established time-out area, and indicate how long the time-out should be. (See "Time-Out Procedure," next page.)
5. Maintain eye contact and a calm voice when speaking to the student.
6. Maintain proximity to the student, but avoid being too close—she may feel her personal space has been compromised.
7. If you feel too irritated or angry to deal with the situation right then, take a time-out yourself. Explain that you need a few minutes and say exactly when you will return to the issue.
8. Invite the student to accompany you outside for a few minutes of fresh air. This allows both of you to get away from the reinforcement of classroom peers.
9. Avoid making such statements as "I know how you feel," which the student may find patronizing. You can only guess.
10. In the heat of the moment, quickly remind yourself that you are the adult and will act like one, no matter how upset you may be. Describe the situation as you see it: "You seem angry. You didn't get what you wanted to play with."

Time-Out Procedure

All students should be taught about the time-out area and the appropriate way to use it.

1. Establish where the time-out area will be. It might be a corner, a carrel, an office, the hall, or a peer's classroom. Location is dependent on the cooperation of other staff as well as the seriousness of the negative behavior. For instance, time-out for a "fight" would be best spent in the office.

2. Ensure that the time-out area has a desk or table and chair and any of the following: soothing music (headphones); a fish tank; a grudge jar (an empty container into which the student can place angry, written thoughts that are later reviewed with the student and either the teacher or counsellor); a tape recorder with a blank tape for recording thoughts (again, reviewed later); a couple of cushions; a supply of plain paper; and a variety of "safe" writing tools, such as pencils and crayons. In addition, provide some tactile tools, such as a soft, squeezable ball, textured materials, fur, and bubble paper (the plastic wrapping paper covered with tiny air bubbles, which children love to pop).

3. Establish for how long at a time a student can use the area. Five minutes is usually enough.

4. Emphasize that the time-out area is for emergency use only.

5. Have a sign-out sheet posted beside the door for students to record the time of leaving the class.

6. Teach the students how to use the time-out area appropriately.
   - Ask for a time-out pass.
   - Write your name on the appropriate paper that indicates exactly when you left the classroom.
   - Go to the time-out area quietly and sit down.
   - Write a brief account of why you are there.
   - If desired, choose one of the available activities.
   - When time is up, return to the room and sign back in.
   - Give your written account to your teacher.

7. Every time a student uses the time-out area, keep a permanent record of who, when, and for how long. This is very important in case you have to report to parents or the principal at a later date.

8. For debriefing, be sure to meet with a student who has used the time-out area sometime that same day.

39. Forming Random Groups
… whether they be for work or for play

"I was in Angie's group last time," whined Tim. *"Why do I have to be in her group again?"*

"You picked the same color as she did, didn't you? Yellow?" replied his teacher.

"Yep. But I didn't want yellow."

"Maybe next time you'll pick a different color from Angie."

"Geez!" Tim slumped off to the Yellow group. *"Luck of the draw!"*

The teacher smiled at his Grade 3 student's response, glad that he had reinforced the Teacher's Choice methods of grouping early in the year.

Ten Ways to Form Random Groups

1. *Odds & Evens:* Count, starting at "1." All the odds go together, as do the evens. Recount within each group, using the same pattern, to form four groups in total.
2. *Alphabet Awareness:* Students take paper tags with a letter of the alphabet on each—there are as many different letters as groups desired. They silently choose a word beginning with the appropriate letter, perhaps *boy* for the letter "B," then move around saying only their word to find others who have words beginning with the same letter. A letter "B" group might be made up of *boy, big, black, butter,* and perhaps a second *boy.* This activity promotes the alphabetic principle and phonemic awareness.
3. *Sweet Talk:* From a bag or container, students randomly pull a piece of wrapped candy, one color or kind representing each group desired. For example, all the red candies signify one group. Once they have formed their groups accordingly, they can eat the candies.
4. *Shakes:* Students draw a tag with a number from a container. Keeping their numbers silent, they move around shaking hands with others—one shake for each number. They form their groups by quickly finding others with the same number of shakes.
5. *Words:* Use words relevant to a topic being studied and as many as you want groups. For example, to create six groups in Science, the words on slips of paper might be *electricity, conduit, amps, wires, negative, positive.* Students draw papers randomly and then locate other students with the same word.
6. *Silent Signals:* Verbs, such as *creep, hop, slide, skip,* and *crawl,* or feeling terms, such as *sad, happy, angry,* and *nervous,* appear on randomly chosen papers to encourage students to behave in a certain way to find their groups.
7. *Happy Families:* Randomly chosen papers identifying family members lead students to their "group families." For example, Mother Smith, Father Smith, Uncle Smith, Sister Smith, and Baby Smith compose one group.
8. *Sing-a-long:* Randomly drawn papers indicate simple songs the students know (e.g., Three Blind Mice). On cue, students move around singing the songs as prompted by the papers and find others singing the same songs.
9. *Switcheroo:* Randomly select as many students as you want groups, for example, five students for five groups, and number the groups. Each student in turn chooses someone from the class. Once you randomly draw a number (1–5), the chosen student goes to the group with that assigned number. No one knows who will end up where.
10. *Q/A:* Pose as many questions on paper as desired groups; having correct answers on paper determines group membership.

Have you ever avoided a group activity because the thought of getting the students into groups was just too much to handle?

Note: Random groups are heterogeneous collections of students brought together for a specific game, activity, project, or task. They are not instructional groups, which are usually determined according to needs.

Note: If you don't want the "sugar," use colored poker chips, tiddlywinks, or small squares of paper.

Note: You can also use new vocabulary or spelling words on the papers.

Ten Tips for Effective Group Functioning

There are two types of groups: casual and instructional. These pointers apply to both.

1. Teach students rules for group behavior. Group members are expected to
    *   share duties and supplies equally
    *   cooperate with one another by using positive language and pleasant voices
    *   take turns listening to other members speak
    *   show respect to one another by being polite and giving positive comments for work well done
    *   help one another with any difficulties experienced
    *   work together to come up with one good idea, presentation, or project
    *   keep personal records of the time spent in the group
2. Decide whether you want homogeneous groups (usually for specific instructional purposes) or heterogeneous groups (usually for activities), and how many students per group. A homogeneous group consists of students with similar needs and abilities; a heterogeneous group, of students with varied abilities and needs.
3. Plan the manner in which you want students to form groups (see Ten Ways to Form Random Groups Easily and Deliberately, above). Prepare any necessary paper slips or colored markers.
4. Establish your expectations. Exactly what do you want the groups to do, where and when? Know the *purpose*.
5. Plan the work area and materials before letting students get into groups.
6. Before groups are formed, provide clear directions, both orally and in written form, set timelines for choosing roles within the group and brainstorming, and establish evaluation procedures for groups and individual group members.
7. If students will play individual roles within each group (leader, illustrator, speaker …), explain the roles and the way in which they will be determined before groups form.
8. Once groups are working, circulate and provide reinforcement.
9. To keep the idea of getting into groups fresh, constantly try innovative ways to accomplish this.
10. Add a competitive element to forming groups, for example, a prize for the first group to find all its members and sit quietly. This not only gets students moving quickly, it adds interest and limits the possibility of complaining about one's group.

Motivation

Not all instructional techniques appeal to all students; not all strategies enable all to learn. Good teachers use a variety of methods so that all students will want to learn *most* of the time. These begin with the establishment of good rapport with students—without this, other motivational tactics may be useless. They also include the daily infusion of humor into the classroom. In a random survey I conducted in several elementary and junior high schools, "good sense of humor" was ranked as very important by all students. In addition to using humor, increasing student accountability works to motivate most students; it demonstrates to them the significance or importance of what they are doing. Using activities based on drama or musical theatre often provides an inherent motivation for students, and for those less "turned on," the effects of positive group pressure work to increase their motivation for the activities. This section includes a variety of teaching ideas that may enable classroom teachers to better influence and engage their students.

Establishing Rapport: Rapport is that wonderful bond that allows teacher and students to work and learn well together. The powerful teacher creates this relationship early in the year and works to maintain it. When good rapport has been established, students and teacher enjoy one another and the class, and students feel more motivated to do well.

Teaching with a Sense of Humor: There are so many powerful benefits to doing this that it would be impossible to list them here. Let me just say that in addition to being a survival tool for teachers, humor is a natural way to enhance teacher–student relationships and create a positive learning environment. Some teachers feel they lack any sense of humor and teach as if this were true. It's not. If you are a teacher, you have a sense of humor. Perhaps you just need to fine-tune it, for most certainly, a sense of humor is developed, not inherited.

Making Lessons Motivating: What is learned or taken away from a lesson is, for most students, directly related to how "turned on" they were to the teacher's presentation. Were they hooked at the beginning? Did they maintain attention throughout? Were they able to recount the facts or major pieces of learning when the lesson was finished? Not all material presented at school is motivating to all students so it's up to the teacher to use often subtle tactics to keep lessons as motivating as possible. The teacher who is able to do this will notice that not only are the students more receptive, but their work and academic successes are greater too. What better motivation could a teacher have to keep lessons motivating?

Raising Accountability: Adults work for rewards: their cheques. Students work for rewards, too; however, not all of them have the intrinsic motivation necessary for school success. Instilling this then becomes the responsibility of the teacher: to somehow make students accountable for their work—not always an easy task. Accountability is a powerful tool. The teacher who increases it in students enjoys more completed work, high-quality work, and more motivated students.

Using Drama Every Day: All children love to play, to pretend, to be active. Teachers can capitalize on this by incorporating brief, planned-for drama activities into the daily routine. Drama fans will recognize these as warm-ups. For the rest of us, they are "focused, purposeful, and powerful energy releasers" that can be added to other activities throughout the day to enhance student involvement and delight.

Involving Students in Musical Theatre: *Musical theatre*, as presented here, means movement, acting, and exploring through music to give a message or tell a story. It can be a spontaneous activity or a choreographed and practised production number. Perhaps the most important reason for its consistent inclusion is that in a very powerful manner, it capitalizes on what children love to do: to move. The teacher who uses musical theatre enjoys happier students and personal satisfaction.

40. Establishing Rapport

… with students

Have you ever been "slightly" jealous of a colleague whom all the students seemed to adore and put on their best behavior for?

Miss Schneider was a first-year teacher. She was excited and nervous about meeting her students for the first time. Would they like her? How would she establish the rapport she knew would be necessary to make the year productive? When the students filed into her room on Day 1, she stood at the door and smiled at each one, asking names and repeating them. The children responded. The first step to good rapport had been easier to make than she had thought.

Ten Ways to Establish Rapport with Students

1. Disclose a little about yourself, providing appropriate information at an appropriate time. Use personally relevant examples in class and have a few personal items, such as photos, in the room.
2. Learn the students' names, and a little about them, as soon as possible. Keep checklists about students' likes, interests, strengths, and so on, so that you can be sincere and specific when talking to them.
3. Show sincerity and humility (students are quick to recognize insincerity). Avoid being arrogant and, if appropriate, be self-deprecating. For example, before a lesson about "responsibility," you may wish to share an experience where you foolishly locked yourself out of your car and had to pay a locksmith to open the door.
4. Make yourself available at times other than in class. Stay after school just to chat.
5. Behave in a warm and friendly way, not only because it helps to establish rapport, but because you want to. Students need to know that you care.
6. Maintain a cheerful attitude, and smile a lot. (See Cheerfulness, page 10.)
7. Always treat students with respect. (See Respect, page 14.)
8. Maintain eye contact and give focus when talking to your students.
9. Watch students closely to get clues about them from their body language.
10. Maintain or cultivate a sense of humor, and use jokes and "in-class silliness" now and then.

41. Teaching with a Sense of Humor
… to spark motivation, rapport, and general interest

Does a particular teacher from your childhood still stand out in your memory? Chances are that teacher had a good sense of humor.

"I love school," eleven-year-old Ross told his surprised mother. This was the first time she had ever heard those words from her usually uninterested and unmotivated son.

"Good," she said. "What's so different about this year?"

"Mr. Davidson," Ross smiled. "He's the best. He always tells jokes and he laughs right along with us when something dumb happens, even when it happens to him. He's cool."

Ten Ways to Build Your Sense of Humor

1. Remind yourself that nothing is ever as serious as we tend to make it. Play the "100 Years" mind game. Ask, "Will it matter 100 years from now?"
2. Buy a few comedy CDs or videos (e.g., Jerry Seinfeld or Ellen DeGeneres). Listening to them will actually improve your sense of humor.
3. Watch at least one comedy show on TV weekly. Choose a good one that will make you laugh out loud.
4. On the way to work, listen to a radio station you find funny, not one that presents the "cold, hard facts." This sets the stage for a more humorous day.
5. Unless you do it well, avoid telling jokes, but do find a few books of good or groaner jokes that you can share with the students. These might include play-on-word or knock-knock joke books. Sometimes, general humor books contain appropriate "kid jokes." Ask the school librarian to help locate these.
6. Try to see the funny side to mundane daily activities. For example, when you are carrying all that "stuff" from your car to the school and you drop something, instead of being annoyed, share this with the students and laugh. Funny things happen every minute of the day.
7. Associate with people who have a good sense of humor and love to laugh. Laughing is contagious, and no one wants to be around a dour person for long.
8. Collect and display humorous posters, cartoons, quotations, and the like. Change them regularly. Consider a Humor bulletin board, where students add their findings regularly, or a Humor unit, next page.
9. Teach with a "twinkle." Everything is as exciting and humorous as you make it through your voice, expression, and enthusiasm.
10. Use humor whenever possible, to defuse potentially "hot" situations. For example, when a student is getting annoyed, say, "Wow! I can feel the heat from here" instead of "Settle down!" The humor helps neutralize the moment.

Humor Unit Ideas

Most teachers prefer to teach units from a thematic point of view. If you use humor as the theme, you can open doors to many wonderful laughs and learnings. Trade books and stories in anthologies that are humorous are easy to find, but sometimes you may not know where to go from there. Here are some ideas for use in the context of a humor unit. Choose ones that interest you and work best with the ages of your students.

• Begin the unit by enthusiastically getting your students to conduct a Humor survey to gather ideas (see next page). This could be used as a hook for the rest of the unit, as the basis for group discussion and sharing, and in any number of creative ways, such as graphing responses, researching the lives of comedians, and researching the connection between laughter and wellness. Students should keep the survey responses for reference throughout the unit.

• Invite students to keep Humor journals in which they record funny happenings, jokes, and more.

• Research puns and their connection to humor.

• Share a joke, then invite students to be prepared to take turns sharing a joke a day.

• Incorporate some "silliness" into an otherwise mundane lesson. For example, have students write a business letter to the supervisor of schools requesting a course in humor for all teachers.

• Invite students to collect humorous sayings from car bumpers. They might choose a favorite and put it into a story or essay, illustrate it, or create a cartoon based on the saying.

• Ask the librarian or check the school library for humorous books, then allow your students to choose from the stock for silent reading.

• Invite students to create humorous self-portraits or Wanted posters.

• In small groups, have students brainstorm for humorous personality traits and create personal Venn diagrams comparing themselves to the traits they have discovered in their groups.

• Have your class watch a funny video without the sound to identify and list humorous nonverbal mannerisms and communication.

• Create an assignment where students collect their ten favorite one-liners. Have a sharing session, either in small groups or with every student telling one joke to the whole class. Discuss why these are funny or not.

Humor Survey

Collect responses from a variety of people.

1. Who is your favorite comedian?

2. Explain what makes that person funny to you.

3. What is your favorite comedy TV show?

4. Explain what makes it funny. Include a few specific examples with your explanation.

5. What is your favorite funny movie?

6. What made it funny? Please provide a few specific examples.

7. Did others like the movie as well as you did? Why or why not?

8. Do you like cartoons or comics? Why or why not?

9. Who do you know in the community, perhaps a relative, neighbor, friend, or coach, who makes you laugh? Describe that person.

10. What is your favorite comic or cartoon? If you don't like any, then which do you think is the worst?

11. Explain your answer to question "10" by including a few specific examples.

12. What are your favorite kinds of jokes? (Examples: Long, narrative, knock-knock, one-liner)

13. Provide three or four examples of these jokes.

14. How many times a day do you think you laugh? (Please circle your response.)

Lots of times	Fairly often	Not much

15. Have you ever laughed until your belly hurt? When and why?

16. Name someone in this school you think is humorous and explain why.

42. Making Lessons Motivating

… so that students' attention stays with the task at hand

How often have you scanned the class only to see that more of the students are not "with you" than are?

Mr. Doherty loved to be different. His students never knew what to expect next. When he entered the room after recess one morning with a sock on each hand, the students were wide eyed. A few giggles could be heard, but the stern look on the teacher's face soon quietened the room. He cleared his throat loudly, then said, "I'd like to introduce you to Mr. X and Mr. Y." He wiggled each hand appropriately. "They are going to teach us by standing for numbers in our math problems today."

"But they're just socks!" one young girl announced.

"Look more closely," Mr. Doherty said seriously. "Use your imaginations. Imagine their funny faces. Mr. X has a pimple on his nose," and he pointed to a hole in one sock, "and Mr. Y is very, very old and wise," and he pointed to the parts of the sock that were threadbare. "Now, let's begin."

Needless to say, the class was a huge success even though occasionally Mr. X had to lie on the teacher's desk while Mr. Doherty wrote on the board.

Ten Ways to Make Lessons Motivating

1. Use "selective silence" or "selective amnesia." Pretend you have lost your voice or your memory and invite students to continue the class by taking turns "teaching."

2. Sometimes, present content through puppets, either commercially or hand made.

3. Let students know, through your stance, voice, and body language, just how important you consider the lesson to be.

4. Make sure that students know exactly why they are doing something and how they will benefit from it. Make some benefits immediate—celebrate small successes.

5. Invite students to come up with mnemonic devices to aid memory of concepts/facts. (*Apostrophe s means not that there's more, but that something belongs to the word just before.*)

6. Use stories, anecdotes, or personal disclosures or deprecations to grab interest at the beginning of a lesson, enhance a point in the middle of a lesson, or close a lesson effectively.

7. Know your students' interests and skills, and use this information to make the lessons relevant to them. For example, if several students like hockey, offer a hockey anecdote or situation in a math problem.

8. Use props whenever possible. More is learned with a "magic wand" than a metre stick as a pointer.

9. Remember that students crave adventure, excitement, and risk. Try to incorporate some of this into lessons. For example, discuss a science project from the "futuristic" point of view and imagine *what if …*

10. Tap into children's natural curiosity by beginning a lesson with a provocative or rhetorical question. (*What would happen if school was closed forever?*)

43. Raising Accountability
… to improve student performance and learning

How often have you thought, "If I could just find some way to get _____ to do his work"?

The parent was pleasantly surprised to see his eleven-year-old son busily working on a science project. Jason wasn't known for being a "good student," and homework had always been a problem. "Good for you, son," he remarked. "Big project?"

"Yeah," Jason mumbled. "Teacher is going to show all of these at the Open House next week."

"Oh," said the father, smiling. So that was it—increased accountability! Good for the teacher! Good for his son!

Ten Ways to Raise Accountability

1. After a group activity, have individuals write or talk about what they contributed or learned.
2. Make activities authentic, purposeful, and connected to real life. (See "Authentic Learning," next page.)
3. Ensure that students see and understand the connection between lessons that prepare for a culminating activity, performance, or product and the final project itself.
4. Show an appropriate level of concern when introducing a task, and provide a timeline for completion.
5. Somewhere in the assignment, task, or work, allow students some measure of responsibility for and control over what they are doing and how they are doing it.
6. Encourage and expect curiosity, perseverance, and good work.
7. Model an activity or share an example of a completed task so that all students know exactly what is expected.
8. Change activities often. Usually, about twenty minutes is sufficient for students in Kindergarten and up to Grade 3, and up to forty minutes for students in Grades 4 to 9.
9. Mark everything, even if that means just initialing an assignment to show you have looked at it. Keep a record of completed assignments and let students know you will be sharing this information with parents.
10. Consider using an Accountability Contract. (See the model on page 78.)

Authentic Learning

- Encourage students to ask questions and make investigations. (Inquiry approach)

- Accept many responses to most questions. (In real life, there are many options.)

- Make use of simulations to practise real-life activities.

- To examine multiple perspectives, create centres, that is, small areas of the room set aside for specific purposes such as writing, reading, or providing practice in new material, usually with a table and a couple of chairs. For example, you might offer a variety of activities related to small businesses, if you were studying small businesses in Social Studies.

- Use the technology students live with: computers. Allow time for experimentation and play.

- Recognize different learning styles by offering choices for tasks and assignment completion, when possible.

- Adopt the publication idea—display or show off as many projects as possible. (Remember to obtain permission.)

- Introduce the discovery method of learning, where students are invited to use trial and error to find things out. Reinforce errors as well as successes.

- Use role playing in a stress-free, low-risk manner—in other words, allow students to "pass"—to develop understanding of self and others.

- Tie literacy experiences to daily living. For example, have students write letters to real people, fill in order forms, and read TV guides.

- Provide a reason or purpose. For example, tell the class that they are going to learn about history to avoid making the same mistakes as people in the past or about propaganda to become more critical purchasers.

Accountability Contract

I, (*student's name*) _____, agree to the following conditions in my

Grade _____ year at (*name of school*) _____

I will, to the best of my abilities,

• come to school on time

• be clean and neat in appearance

• have all my books and materials with me, so I am prepared to work

• do my homework regularly

• respect my teachers and peers

• do my best work always

• follow the school rules

Comments:

_____

_____

_____

_____

Note: Failure to comply with the contract on a regular basis may necessitate seeing the school counsellor or arranging for a parent–teacher conference.

Student Signature _____ Date _____

Teacher Signature _____ Date _____

Parent/Guardian Signature _____ Date _____

44. Using Drama Every Day

… to facilitate learning in all other subject areas

How many times have you said to yourself, "I just don't understand why they don't get it. What more can I do?"

The principal, on his way down the hall, stopped to watch a Grade 2 class in action. The students were rapidly forming and reforming groups in what appeared to be an exciting game. Assuming the class was just "getting rid of steam," he later asked the teacher to confirm his predictions.

"Oh, they were doing that," she assured him, "but they were doing math also. They were playing Atom, a game about addition and subtraction."

The principal shook his head in amazement and wondered if perhaps he was getting too old for his job.

Ten Ways to Use Drama Every Day

1. *Atom:* Students walk in a central area and form groups of whatever number the teacher calls. Those without the correct number are eliminated. (Math)

2. *In-seat mirror imaging:* Partners face each other. One of them, the leader, moves hands and arms slowly and the other follows by maintaining eye contact only. They later change roles. (Science—careful observation)

3. *Milling:* Students move, or mill, in an open space while following cues such as "walk tiredly," "walk on hot stones." (Language Arts—setting a story; Social Studies—conditions of life in some places)

4. *Tableaux:* Small groups create frozen pictures of story scenes, incidents from Social Studies, or math problems (e.g., for 5 – 3 = 2, there might be two students standing rigid, linked together in some way, with three holding frozen poses, such as leaning out and backs turned, to show that they are moving away).

5. *Inner dialogue:* In groups, students discuss a situation (from a narrative, social scene, or even a math problem). Students take on the roles of different characters (or numbers). When tapped on the shoulder, a student speaks inner thoughts in character, for example, *I am the number 10! I am the biggest here so I feel happy.*

6. *Juxtaposition:* Groups display different interpretations of the same situation, for example, a barn raising. In one group, a student could show anger through facial expression and body language because he'd hit his thumb with a nail, another could seem excited as her new barn goes up, another could look serious because he was in charge, and so on; the second group will have entirely different interpretations. Groups usually begin by miming, then adding sounds and talk, if desired. Debriefing helps students see how people react differently in much the same situations.

7. *Mental pictures:* Several students hold a tableau (or interconnected position) for five seconds. Others try to return them to the exact position or to mimic the position. (memory enhancement)

8. *Choral speech:* As a whole class or in groups, students create chants to help learn a difficult concept. (*Dividing fractions is kind of dumb. First, you flip the second one. When it has done a flippity-flop, then multiply across the top.*)

9. *For & Against:* The whole class or groups divide into For and Against sides, then carry out a debate-type argument in support of their position.

10. *Interactive drama:* The reader reads a line of prose or poetry with expression and the students mimic it exactly—very motivating for shy or quiet students.

45. Involving Students in Musical Theatre

... to motivate students and provide alternative ways of learning

Have you ever wondered how to bring a particular scene in a book to life for the students, in a way that was natural and motivating for them?

Note: Musical theatre, as I am discussing it here, can be anything from moving around the classroom to music to "acting out" a story to music, to creating a production piece complete with song and choreographed dance.

Note from a Grade 4 Parent:

Dear Mrs. Laurier,

Jason has never liked school until this year and I think he likes it now because of all the musical theatre he keeps telling me about. I don't exactly know what that is, but he comes home every day eager to share what he's done. Today he told me he acted the part of the wolf in Little Red Riding Hood, and had to "move to music." He was really proud. Thank you for turning Jason on to learning.

Ten Ways to Involve Students in Musical Theatre

1. Begin by asking students to listen, with eyes closed, to selected music, then prompt them to "keep the rhythm." (*Clap, tap, stomp, ...*)
2. Invite students to keep the rhythm while sitting at desks, in any creative manner they can think of. (For example, they might sway, use their hands to make figure eights, or raise or lower their arms.) Let them take turns mimicking each other's movements.
3. Have students keep the rhythm while walking, marching, skipping, or generally moving around the room in either a line (where the first person decides the movement and others copy) or randomly.
4. Invite students to create their own locomotor and hand movements to accompany a piece of music. (Pay attention to any "good" movements they exhibit and discuss these later.)
5. Watch video or DVD selections of movement to music (figure skating, dance routines, choral groups with "actions," cheerleading squads).
6. Add dialogue, words, chants, even nonsense chants (*Do da la me oh*) to a movement that the whole class repeats.
7. Tell or read a story with high action. Stop at an appropriate part and invite students to *predict* what might happen next by moving to a piece of appropriate music. (Classical music, such as *Ride of the Valkyries* and the *William Tell Overture*, often works well.)
8. Begin choreographing a production piece by asking, "Who has a particular movement that works well to this part of the music?" If no suggestions are made, either offer a simple one or point out a movement you have previously noticed. (*I saw ___ moving his arms like this ...*)
9. Divide the class into small random groups (see Forming Random Groups, page 67), play one piece of music, and allow each group to create movements to show the whole class. Discuss the contrast and perhaps the similarity between what the groups produce and possibly choose one movement from each group to combine into a whole-class series of movements.
10. Follow a musical theatre activity by debriefing and calling for written reflections.

Why Try Musical Theatre?

- It is easily used with extreme population diversity (cultural, intellectual, religious, ESL …) because music is a universal theme.

- It is a natural medium for encouraging communication. The class can discuss the music, as well as movements and personal feelings.

- It provides equal, non-threatening, low-risk opportunities for all students, whether they are shy, self-conscious, or extroverted.

- It works in a cross-curricular manner: it can be used in Music, Language Arts, Art, Physical Education, Social Studies, or Math.

- It can be used to introduce or close units, pieces of literature, or generalized themes.

- It is an effective re-focuser, a way to regain students' interest and attention.

- It can be "practised" and used as a production number for concerts, Open Houses, or in-class presentations.

- It provides a way to make meaning or clarify a concept.

- For literature, it provides another extension of understanding. Students act out the plot to appropriate music.

- Students love choreographed, or pre-planned and practised, movement as it makes them feel "a part of something important."

- Any teacher can do musical theatre—it is unnecessary to be a dancer or to have previous experience. Just provide the music and the prompts (*Move the way the trees in the story were moving*)—the students will do the rest. Pick a few of the moves made naturally by some students, then teach the entire group the same movements.

Note: The best high school rendition of *West Side Story* that I ever saw was choreographed entirely by a teacher without theatre, dance, or music background. She said she just asked the students to try out moves until they found ones they all liked.

Presentation

Teachers are performers; the classrooms, their stages. Every day they take a variety of stances and approaches, and present ideas and strategies, all of which must be done with enthusiasm and passion. Big as that task is, they are called to do more: to show creativity and flexibility. Finally, they must exercise all of these wonderful traits within an aura of humility.

Cultivating Creativity: Teachers are always told to teach creatively, but seldom told how. Unfortunately, there is an assumption that only a few talented teachers can teach creatively. Not true. Anyone can tap into the power of creativity with only minor adjustments to existing lessons. Creative teaching makes learning fun, instructing easier, morale higher, and students more motivated, attentive, and determined.

Demonstrating Enthusiasm: As you know, enthusiasm is contagious. The most powerful people throughout history have acted with enthusiasm. Similarly, the most powerful teachers exude enthusiasm, and their efforts can be directly correlated with those of their students. Enthusiastic teachers inspire both enthusiasm and confidence in their students.

Showing Flexibility: Flexible teachers take changes to carefully prepared plans in their stride. Although they understand the need for good preparation, they are energized by the "teachable moment" and by the idea of spontaneous learning. Such teachers can change direction without notice and become involved in the excitement of a new learning—a powerful ability when it comes to teaching.

Teaching with Passion: The teacher who is truly passionate about teaching "lights up" in the classroom. Passion goes further than enthusiasm in that it spreads to even the most mundane areas of teaching. The passionate teacher is always excited about everything from lesson planning to supervision. It's a state of mind—a way of being powerful—that separates this teacher from those who are just surviving. Lucky are the students who are exposed to someone with a passion for teaching because they will become excited about learning and have more fun and pleasure in class.

Practising Humility: Humility in teaching means recognizing and accepting professional strengths while understanding that they are to be used on behalf of the students. Humble teachers knows their importance to the lives of their students and can fully see and appreciate student strengths and accomplishments. Humility may well be the finest indicator of successful teaching.

46. Cultivating Creativity

… in teaching style and behavior

How often have you wished you were as creative as someone else? (Chances are that person has had to work at creativity too!)

The Grade 8 class was restless. It was the last week before winter break and no one wanted to do math. The teacher thought for a moment, then announced enthusiastically, "Who wants to play Simon Says?"

"But we're too old," one student protested suspiciously.

"Never!" the teacher replied and stepped on a chair so all could see him clearly. "Stand up everyone!"

And they did. After a few hilarious minutes, the class settled down to at least attempt the math.

Ten Ways to Cultivate Creativity

1. Pay attention to what delights students. Think like a kid! Ask yourself, *If I was a student in my class, what would excite me or help me to learn this concept?* Imagine how a six-year-old would see a particular situation.

2. Keep an idea book handy all the time. Jot down any good ideas you see on TV or in magazines, encyclopedias, science fiction books, catalogues, movies, and environmental print. A good resource is *99 Activities and Greetings,* by Melissa Correa-Connolly (Pembroke Publishers).

3. Constantly look for ideas that have worked for others. Attend teacher-training sessions and swap ideas with as many other teachers as possible.

4. Use as many different approaches to teaching as possible, for example, audio-visuals, overheads, charts, game playing, dramatizations, singing, and chanting, in an adventurous and enthusiastic way.

5. Know your subjects as well as possible. Teaching creatively depends on first feeling confident in skills and subject-knowledge.

6. Expose yourself to as many creative endeavours as possible. Listen to good music; attend theatre; visit art galleries and museums.

7. Allow yourself to "act creative" once in a while. Do whatever this means to you, perhaps dressing in funky fashion. Risk taking promotes creativity; you will feel—and act—more creative.

8. Use the power of the unconscious mind. Mentally describe a challenge before going to sleep or for a long, quiet walk and allow your mind to brainstorm for ideas. It will!

9. Tell yourself that there is a place for "silly" in the classroom. Allow yourself, at times, to be child-like and playful.

10. As a way to promote your personal creativity, pick one negative incident, such as a student outburst in class, and think of five reasons why it was "good." Then mentally list all the creative things you did in the past week.

47. Demonstrating Enthusiasm

… in your teaching and with your profession

Have you ever wondered how the actors in a stage play that lasts for years continue to demonstrate enthusiasm every single night? It's because they are actors—and so are teachers.

Taken from a Junior High survey, "What Makes a Good Teacher?":

- *Someone who is really excited to be teaching us*
- *Our teacher because he loves to teach math*
- *I think a good one loves kids and loves his job.*
- *A teacher who does cool things to make us want to learn and is real sort of sparkly in class all the time*

Ten Ways to Demonstrate Enthusiasm

1. Use body language to your advantage. Show enthusiasm by first feeling it, then standing erect, rather than relaxed, and exuding it.
2. Speak briskly using a variety of modulations and tones in your voice. Listen to your voice on a tape recording to check this.
3. Maintain eye contact when speaking, and smile often.
4. Act energetically, regardless of how you feel. When you radiate energy, even when you are tired and have to "pretend," the results will be well worth the effort.
5. Think of someone who is enthusiastic and emulate that person's behavior.
6. Develop a curiosity about your students, your courses, and life in general. Ask questions to show your interest.
7. View difficult situations more as challenges for growth than as problems.
8. Treat yourself to something special every day—a fresh flower, a delicious coffee, a five-minute walk.
9. Celebrate everything possible, such as birthdays, improved marks, behaviors, and special days. The celebrations need not be big; often a word or two will do.
10. Substitute "could" instead of "should" and "will" instead of "can't" in your daily activities and thoughts.

48. Showing Flexibility

… of attitude and behavior in the classroom

Have you ever regretted not allowing an interesting diversion your class wanted to take and insisted on "sticking to the curriculum" instead?

The teacher noticed immediately that one group was completely off-task. Instead of using math manipulatives to figure out the addition and subtraction problems, they were busy building a precarious-looking tower with the small blocks. She quickly decided to allow them to continue with their construction, then invite them to share how they overcame the danger of the tower toppling. Not math exactly— but a worthwhile pursuit nevertheless. They could do the math problems later.

Ten Ways to Show Flexibility

1. Present information in many different ways, for a variety of purposes.
2. Encourage students to take active roles in their learning, to share perspectives, and to ask "why?"
3. Accept multiple solutions to problems.
4. Exchange classes with a peer teacher for a day (or a subject).
5. Become involved in the mind–body culture by taking yoga classes. There is a correlation between physical flexibility and cognitive flexibility.
6. Rearrange your classroom; put your desk in an unusual location.
7. Invite the students to plan and take charge of a class. Understand that there is a certain messiness to good teaching, and encourage divergence from the norm.
8. Prepare a lesson plan, then refrain from looking at it again; go with the flow of the class.
9. Skip a regular class, such as "math at 10 a.m. daily," and do something different. For instance, take the class for a brisk walk or allow them to listen to a beautiful poem or piece of music.
10. Periodically alter your personal routine. For example, instead of morning coffee, have hot chocolate; rather than eating breakfast on the run, stop for a full breakfast.

Ways to Stretch Your Lessons

- Change directions.
- Adapt as you go.
- Encourage divergent thinking.
- Accept alternative ideas.
- Skip or repeat sections.

---

49. Teaching with Passion

… for your profession and for the instruction of your students

How often have you thought, "I'm too tired today. I just can't face them"?

The school year was over. Most of the Junior High students had fled the premises, filled with the joy of summer holidays and the expectation of lazy days ahead. But one class was still filled with eager faces—not only those of Mr. Park's own class, but of other classes, as well. They stayed for ages—apparently reluctant to leave. As the last of them finally exited the building, the principal asked about this curious phenomenon.

"Oh, we stay because Mr. Park is so cool," the girl replied. "He's so enthusiastic about everything and he's always made learning fun. He teaches with passion!"

The principal was amazed. "Out of the mouths of babes …," he thought.

Ten Ways to Teach with Passion

1. Strive to be a "glass half full" type of teacher—even if things are not going as planned. Smiles are contagious and they make the person who is smiling feel better too.
2. Maintain a high level of commitment to keeping abreast of the latest technology, information, and instructional strategies in your field. It's hard to be passionate about teaching something you find unfamiliar.
3. Set realistic goals for yourself as a teacher and strive to reach them; then, be sure to celebrate little successes daily.
4. Have passion for the subject you are teaching; remind yourself constantly of the many wonderful and rewarding reasons you chose your profession and consider yourself lucky to have the opportunity to share exciting subject material with young minds. If you are passionate about the subject, it will show in the way you teach it.
5. Consider yourself an actor with the lead role in a huge performance—the classroom is your stage. Strive to deliver your *best* performance every day.
6. Keep the gusto in your voice. Even the most mundane lesson will be accepted with enthusiasm if your voice delivers it with excitement and passion. Audiotape yourself teaching for a quick voice check.
7. Celebrate the joy of teaching. Look for all the perks and positives of your profession and focus on these each day to and from school.
8. Let the students know you care—about them, about learning, and about life. Let them know too that you have faith in their abilities to succeed at all three! A good way to do this is to make yourself approachable to them—an open door usually means an open heart.
9. Remember that your students come first: before marking, planning, or rushing home at dismissal.
10. Maintain your health by getting enough rest. If you feel tired, it's impossible to be passionate about anything.

50. Practising Humility

… in all that you do as an educator

Have you ever created a "class display," maybe a bulletin board or stage presentation, more for the accolades you will receive than for the "good of the children"?

It was a curious situation. Ms. Ladd's class was always "presenting" and the other staff members never ceased to be amazed at the work. The students did skits for assemblies. They decorated all the bulletin boards in the halls. They consistently filled the display case near the office with creative endeavours. But Ms. Ladd's students were more often than not restless, disruptive, off-task, and generally less than happy.

It took the principal almost a year to determine the problem: too much "Ms. Ladd Presents" and not enough child-centred activities. Ms. Ladd, in her eagerness to look good among peers, had been pushing her Grade 3 class to constantly "prepare and present," whether they wanted to or not, and had been reaping the rewards of the students' labors.

Ten Ways of Practising Humility at School

1. Know your place. You are a teacher—not the school principal, psychologist, reading specialist, custodian, secretary, or public health nurse. Avoid "stepping on the toes" of parents, peers, superiors, or support staff.
2. Use the words "Is it possible …" when questioning a student or colleague, rather than inadvertently suggesting you know more than they do with statements such as "You did … incorrectly."
3. Admit mistakes quickly. It takes humility to ask for help.
4. Consistently remind yourself that you could be wrong. After all, no one is perfect.
5. Avoid letting the power of your position go to your head. Remember that in your teaching successes, you are still indebted to the students.
6. Show patience and respect all the time.
7. Look for and acknowledge the good in others.
8. Model humility, but never put yourself down or allow anyone to treat you with any form of disrespect.
9. Avoid over-humble statements such as "Thank you for taking a few minutes from your hectic schedule." Many people find this irritating.
10. Accept accolades or reinforcements in a simple, direct manner. For example, say, "Thank you," rather than "Oh, I don't deserve this."

A Model for Humility

I am …

- important, but not indispensable
- valued, but not invaluable
- powerful, but not omnipotent

Leadership

A teacher's job is one of leadership. The very term *leadership* implies an awareness of where to go and how to get there. In order to be good leaders, teachers are advised to put their students in the context of Maslow's Hierarchy of Needs (see below). They will come to understand that the higher needs become motivating only if the lower needs are being met. In other words, before guiding the students through instruction addressing cognitive or even aesthetic needs, to lead with power, teachers must ensure that their students' needs for physical survival, safety, belongingness and love, and esteem are met. Once these needs are met, though, it is important for teachers to know their objectives for each student and to be able to act on them.

Maslow's Hierarchy of Needs

In addition to everyday in-class leadership, teachers deal with the more difficult areas of tutoring, supervising, counselling, leading students toward responsible behavior, and contributing to extracurricular activities. I offer suggestions for these specific areas of leadership, as I have found that sometimes teachers feel less than adequate in them.

Tutoring Students Effectively: No one knows the students' needs as well as the homeroom teacher does, so it makes sense for that person to provide tutorials. The effectiveness of teacher-as-tutor lies in the undivided attention the student receives for a brief period of time. Given the many demands on teacher time, we need to know and make use of the ways to use tutorial time resourcefully. The teacher who uses tutorial time wisely enjoys more student success and rapport with students, less fatigue, and fewer stragglers.

Handling Supervision Well: Teachers all have to supervise, so why not make it part of teaching well and influencing students? Supervising need not be a low point of the day, but rather a time to improve rapport with students, get a breath of fresh air, and enjoy a change of pace from the regular classroom activities. It's all in how the task is seen. Start a game or simply walk and talk with students—consider supervising an excellent opportunity to hone your leadership skills.

Teaching Students Responsibility: As every teacher knows, there will still be the lost pencils, books, assignments, and so on, but if we focus on the teaching of responsibility, at least some of the students will come out ahead. The teacher whose students become more responsible enjoys more student time on task, more self-confidence in students, and a greater sense of peacefulness.

Counselling Carefully: Teachers know that being a counsellor to their students is just one of the many hats they wear every day. What they may not know is just how important that role is to the students or how powerful they are when wearing a counsellor's hat. Students trust their teachers; they spend a great deal of time with these important adults and are often more willing to confide in them than in anyone else. Consequently, it behoves teachers to take the counselling role seriously.

Leading Extracurricular Activities: Extracurricular activities benefit not only the school as a whole, but the involved teachers as well. This is where the students can be viewed in an entirely different light, where rapport can be established, and where positive-image visibility and leadership skills are highlighted. Although the time commitment may seem daunting, teachers can give as little or as much time as they want, and the paybacks are worth every minute. Have fun! Consider this a perk of the profession, not a drawback.

51. Tutoring Students Effectively

... on a daily basis as well as for specific one-to-one sessions

Have you ever asked a student to stay after school for help but afterward felt it was a total waste of time?

"I need help." Famous last words, heard frequently by teachers. Miss Jordan had agreed to meet with Stephanie and Melissa after school to help them with their research reports, but the time was dragging and although the girls had been working for almost an hour, little had been accomplished. Finally letting the girls go, Miss Jordan decided she needed a new approach to tutorials: one that would work and use time well.

Ten Ideas to Promote Effective Tutoring

1. Personally invite the student(s) to the tutorial, as this reflects your level of concern. I have used little invitation cards with the exact time, place, date, and reason for the tutorial.

2. Give the student the choice of attending or not, and in your letter home, make clear to families that participation is voluntary. Mandatory tutorials usually do not work.

3. Establish a consistent time and place for the tutorials. It is often better (more "professional" seeming to students) to use some neutral place, such as a desk in the library or office, rather than your classroom.

4. Ensure that you won't be interrupted during the tutorial. Turn off your cellphone, inform the secretary to hold your calls, and hang a "do not disturb" sign on the door.

5. Plan ahead of time what you hope to accomplish and bring necessary materials.

6. Begin by asking the student(s) what the perceived concerns or needs are.

7. Compare these to your own concerns for the student, and decide together on a plan of action. (*Today we will cover ... We'll meet again next Tuesday to do ...*)

8. Establish a time frame of one half hour and stick to it. Students will not appreciate being kept longer than they expected.

9. Right after the session, record what happened, how long you worked, and what pertinent details came from the tutorial.

10. Send home a letter to parents or guardians *before* you begin tutoring, explaining what and why and assuring them that their child has chosen this extra help. Include the exact date, time, and place of the session(s) and invite their questions and comments. Let them know the best times and ways to contact you.

52. Handling Supervision Well

… at recess, noon, or before or after school

Have you ever been guilty of forgetting your supervision duties? How often have you thought that your life as a teacher would be better if you didn't have to supervise?

The teachers in the staff room always wondered why Mr. Day seemed to be the only teacher who enjoyed supervision. Eventually, they asked him.

"Oh, it's easy," he replied. "I don't consider it supervision. I consider it my personal time to get to know a few students better. I don't have time during the rest of the day, so I look forward to this special time with them."

Ten Ways to Handle Supervision Well

1. Highlight your supervision days on your large desk calendar to avoid forgetting them.
2. Write your supervision times directly into your weekly lesson plans.
3. Determine ahead of time which student(s) you would like to approach to improve rapport; then, actively seek them out while you are supervising.
4. Circulate and greet as many students as possible. Take this special opportunity to see them in a different light.
5. Refrain from carrying a coffee cup. The cup sets a barrier between you and the students—they don't carry them—and may negatively affect your ability to build relationships.
6. Supervise where you are supposed to when you are supposed to. You thereby model responsibility for the students.
7. Dress comfortably on supervision days, paying special attention to your footwear.
8. To some degree, take part in games and activities. Students react more favorably to teachers who "play" with them.
9. Watch out for loners and seek them out, even if they are not in your homeroom.
10. Use this time to praise and affirm students that you may have overlooked during the day. (*That was a great job you did yesterday on the math quiz. I could tell you studied because you …*)

53. Teaching Students Responsibility

… in school as well as in life

Have you ever watched a child lose her book for the tenth time and wondered how someone so irresponsible would ever get through life?

"Teacher, can I use your pencil?"
 "Where's yours?"
 "Dunno."
 "But I just gave you a pencil two minutes ago."

Ten Ways to Teach Students Responsibility

1. Provide concise, easily understood directions and expectations. (See Providing Clear Directions, page 55.) Avoid repeating directions many times, thereby shifting to them the responsibility for listening and acting accordingly

2. Ensure that every student has some personal space (locker, desk, box) and regularly provide time to organize and clean up the space.

3. Encourage the use of homework books, daily logs, or journals for recording work done and work to be done. Increase the desire to be responsible in this area by giving marks for upkeep. Keep in mind individual differences and learning styles, though. Some students do less well with this kind of task than others so should be given more help to write in their books. Also, be sure to provide "class" time for recording.

4. Incorporate a buddy system, where partners are responsible for keeping each other "on track" with homework, assignments, and more.

5. Explicitly teach a lesson on responsible behavior. Read stories, such as *The Three Questions* by Jon J. Muth or almost any Robert Munsch book, and write about the topic. Ask the school librarian for other titles.

6. Make a wall chart "Responsible Behaviors." Points might include being prepared with books, pencils, and other supplies; cleaning up after yourself; showing good manners to everyone; accepting responsibility for your actions; and attending school or class on time.

7. Regularly acknowledge responsible behavior in the classroom. (*Today Billy had two pencils for math. Good for you, Billy!*)

8. Provide enough structure on a daily basis that students know what to expect when; then, expect them to be prepared.

9. Send notes home and to the principal acknowledging responsible behaviors that you have noted in the school.

10. Send the students on a Responsible Behavior Scavenger Hunt. Their focus is to watch for and record anything that they deem to be responsible behavior. Discuss in class.

Responsible Behaviors
- **Being prepared** with books, pencils and whatever is needed
- **Cleaning up** after yourself
- **Using good manners** with *everyone*
- **Accepting responsibility** for what you have done
- **Being on time** for school or class

54. Counselling Carefully

… on a day-to-day basis as well as in special circumstances

How often have you thought you spend more time counselling and managing behavior than teaching?

Jenna, abnormally quiet all day, looked upset. Finally, her teacher, Mrs. Smith, took her aside and quietly asked the girl if she was unhappy about something and would like to talk to the school counsellor.

"No," Jenna mumbled.

"She may be able to help you," Mrs. Smith added.

"No, I mean, I don't want to speak to the counsellor," Jenna clarified. "I want to talk with you. The counsellor doesn't even know me."

Ten-Point Procedure for Counselling Students Carefully

1. Sit facing the student, at eye level, with your body in a relaxed, open position (leaning slightly forward, hands relaxed).
2. Wait for a few seconds before saying anything to allow the student time to reflect.
3. Initial prompts might include comments relating to what you have witnessed, such as, "You seem upset" or "You were very quiet today."
4. Further prompts should be "I" statements that paraphrase or summarize the student's words. Examples include "I think you are saying …", "I hear you saying you want …"
5. If the student begins to describe something that you feel you will need to report to the principal, interrupt quickly and explain your position. Legally you are required to report any incident related to child abuse.
6. Except for reports of child abuse, assure the student of the confidentiality of your talk. Maintain it at all costs.
7. Help the student formulate a plan for dealing with the situation. Ensure that the child has some form of action to take right away.
8. Plan another time to get together to recheck the situation.
9. Summarize the session for the student.
10. Immediately after the session, record what happened.

55. Leading Extracurricular Activities

… as this is, to some degree, expected of every teacher

When the principal announced that all staff members were expected to be involved in an extracurricular activity, Ms. White cringed. Away from her Grade 1 class, she felt uncomfortable and ineffective. An extracurricular activity could involve those big Grade 6 kids, couldn't it? One of her colleagues suggested she start a poetry club. It would be easy, he said. It would also be fun. He was right. After only a few Poetry Club meetings, Ms. White felt right at home—even with the Grade 6'ers—and the Poetry Club was a huge success!

Ten Extracurricular Activities*

1. *School Newsletter Club:* Members put together a "booklet" newsletter, sent home, perhaps monthly. The newsletter may include snapshots, samples of student writing, reports on past events, information about upcoming events, and more.

2. *Memory Book Club:* The club produces a school photo album representing the whole year. The album stays in the library for all to enjoy.

3. *The Survey Club:* In this club, students conduct regular surveys through interviews or questionnaires relating to "hot topics" in the school. (*Should we have a lunch room? Should we get longer recesses? Should there be a pop machine?*) Results are compiled, written up, and presented at assemblies.

4. *The Entertainment Club:* Monthly, the club sponsors a special event, such as an afternoon tea, bake sale, storytelling extravaganza, or poetry reading, and invites different groups—a particular grade, another school, nearby seniors, all the staff—to attend.

5. *The Helping Hand Club:* Students provide "help" in the local community, raking leaves, shovelling snow, and picking up garbage. They may also serve neighborhood facilities, such as a local daycare centre, seniors' residence, or their own school. Sometimes, large supermarkets enjoy help from eager students too.

6. *Readers & Scribes Club:* These students lend their reading eyes and writing hands to those unable to do these tasks for themselves. They can visit seniors' homes, daycare centres, Kindergarten and Grade 1 classes, hospitals, and community members requiring living assistance.

7. *The Catering Club:* As a group, they plan, prepare, and present healthy snacks for each monthly staff meeting. They may "cater" other special school events, such as Open House or parent–teacher conferences, too.

8. *Class Yearbook Club:* Students collect writings, illustrations, reviews of events, and so on, to collate into a class yearbook. Either one copy per student is made, or a single master copy remains in the class. (Usually every student wants one and a minimal fee can be collected to cover paper costs.)

9. *The Catalogue Club:* This group records and catalogues everything from extra desks and outdated library books to student offers to do yard clean-up. Periodically, it sends out a flyer to the community, neighboring schools, and businesses.

10. *The Tutoring Club:* Members are taught how to tutor peers or younger students and are sent off to tutor. At regular meetings, they report problems and successes and discuss new strategies.

*Other than the familiar coaching and drama clubs

Have you ever thought you couldn't possibly be involved in extracurricular activities because you had no talents or hobbies worth sharing?

Before you begin an extracurricular activity new to your school, remember to advise your principal, get approval, and then promote your club.

How to Promote Your Club

- illustrated posters in school and community
- flyers hand delivered to each classroom
- a small advertisement in a local newspaper
- a cheery note in the school newsletter
- a banner outside your classroom
- personal invitations
- a brief speech at an assembly

Afterword

A student once asked me if I liked being a teacher. I quickly assured her I did. Then she asked, "Why?" Slightly surprised, I promptly replied, "Because of you—all of you—the students." She nodded and walked away, apparently satisfied with that answer. As she left the room, I realized the significance of what I had said.

I am sure that, as teachers, you will agree that we are "there" for our students; it is also true, though, that our students are there for us. Every day they sit in our classes waiting to be influenced, empowered, nurtured, and taught well. Their trust in our capabilities as educators, mentors, leaders, and imparters of knowledge justifies all the effort that we put into our pursuit of excellence in teaching. Our students deserve teachers who exhibit personal and professional power over themselves and over their teaching capabilities. It is for our students that we hone our skills, develop the personal traits that enable us to fulfill our jobs better, and strive to be the best teachers possible.

It is my hope that the ideas in this book will help you to reach these lofty goals and thereby better meet the needs of your students. In so doing, you will not only be a powerful teacher, but you will experience the ultimate joy of our profession: watching children grow and develop. As Ben Sweetland beautifully states, "We cannot hold a torch to light another's path without brightening our own." I hope you can use *55 Teaching Dilemmas* to brighten your path as well as those of your students.

Index